30 DAYS TO
Taming
YOUR
Fears

Deborah Smith Pegues

HARVEST HOUSE PUBLISHERS

EUGENE, OREGON

30 Days to Taming Your Fears
Copyright © 2011 by Deborah Smith Pegues
Published by Harvest House Publishers
Eugene, Oregon 97402
www.harvesthousepublishers.com

ISBN 978-0-7369-2041-4 (pbk.)
ISBN 978-0-7369-4140-2 (eBook)

Printed in the United States of America

11 12 13 14 15 16 17 18 / BP-NI / 10 9 8 7 6 5 4 3 2 1

*This book is dedicated to every reader
who will decide to take authority
over the spirit of fear and lead a
more peaceful and productive life.*

Contents

Acknowledgments. 7

Prologue: Anxieties, Fears, and Phobias 9

Part 1: Health and Safety Fears

1. Fear of Dying. 17
2. Fear of Doctors and Needles 23
3. Fear of Becoming Disabled 29
4. Fear of Creepy, Crawly Things 35
5. Fear of Dogs. 39
6. Fear of Enclosed Spaces 45
7. Fear of Heights 49
8. Fear of Flying. 53
9. Fear of Drowning 57
10. Fear of Natural Disasters 61
11. Fear of Terrorism 67
12. Fear of Crime and Violence. 71

Part 2: Relational Fears

13. Fear of Loneliness. 77
14. Fear of Commitment 83
15. Fear of Intimacy 89
16. Fear of Rejection. 93

17. Fear of Losing a Loved One............ 99
18. Fear of Social Situations................ 105

Part 3: Psychological Fears

19. Fear of Inadequacy..................... 111
20. Fear of Public Speaking 115
21. Fear of Gaining Weight 123
22. Fear of Aging.......................... 129
23. Fear of Helplessness or Losing Control 135
24. Fear of Change and Letting Go........... 141
25. Fear of Failure......................... 147

Part 4: Financial Fears

26. Fear of Success........................ 155
27. Fear of Lack.......................... 161
28. Fear of Losing a Job 165
29. Fear of Investing or Losing Money........ 171
30. Fear of Retiring Poor 177

Epilogue: Neutralize Your Fear...Get Your
    Life in Gear 183
Appendix 1: Fear-Fighting Scriptures 187
Appendix 2: Fear-Banishing Prayer 191
Notes.................................. 193

Acknowledgments

I offer special thanks to my friends at Zoe Christian Fellowship (ZCF) of Whittier, California, for their prayers and support of this project: Pastor Edward and Vanessa Smith, Kelvin and Delisa Kelley, Ralph and Cathy Lawson, Michael and Lois Douglas, Ronald and Redelia Fowler, and the entire ZCF family.

I am indebted to Roberta Morris and Diane Gardner who unselfishly offered their time and talent to review the manuscript; their input was invaluable. Billie Rodgers, Belinda Wallace, Cheryl Martin, Alvin and Pam Kelley, John Patton, Carol Pegues, and Creola Waters played a critical role through their prayers, input, and inspiration. I am extremely grateful for the following family members whose support facilitated my writing schedule: Rube and Gina Smith, Bobby Smith, and Gene Smith.

My Harvest House dream team continues to stoke the fires of inspiration. Thanks to President Bob Hawkins for your humility and leadership, acquisitions editor Terry Glaspey for your endless ideas and motivation, senior editor Rod Morris for your passion for correct interpretation and application of the Scriptures, and the entire staff for your commitment to excellence.

Finally, the faithfulness and support of my loving husband, Darnell, is a testimony of God's goodness.

Prologue

Anxieties, Fears, and Phobias

As I write this, it's been five nights since my husband, Darnell, left for Kansas City to visit his ailing brother; however, it seems much longer because I've spent each night alone in our home—a major accomplishment for me in over thirty-two years of marriage! Until now, I just couldn't bring myself to do it. The fact that we'd had a burglary a few years ago only added to my apprehension. At the time, I thought I would always experience anxiety when entering our home—especially the master bedroom from which major items had been stolen. However, by the grace of God, I took immediate and proactive steps to overcome my fear and have enjoyed many restful nights since—with Darnell by my side of course.

Now, when I decided to write a book on how to tame fears, I thought it would be downright hypocritical to proclaim life-changing principles and strategies on how to neutralize fears and not practice them myself. So, for the sake of integrity and my own deliverance, here I sit... home alone...late at night. So far so good.

Darnell is due back tomorrow. I've already resisted

the temptation to work all night over the past few days to avoid going to bed during the hours of darkness. I also did not ask a friend to stay with me, nor did I choose to spend the time at one of my many relatives. While I have had a few bouts of nighttime anxiety, I have already declared my victory since my goal was not to allow fear to dictate my behavior. I now know that I can and will stay home alone again when Darnell has to leave town—for I was not alone. I have meditated on and recited Psalm 91:11 so many times over the past five nights that a scan of my brain would probably show these words: "For he will command his angels concerning you to guard you in all your ways" (NIV).

Fear is perhaps the oldest emotion known to mankind. Over the years, it has often been my greatest friend—and my greatest enemy. I was raised in a strict Pentecostal environment in the Deep South. My pastor, parents, and Sunday school teachers constantly warned that Jesus could return to the earth at any moment to "catch away" His people. They cautioned that anyone He found committing any kind of sin would face eternal damnation; there would be no mercy. When I went away to college and experienced freedom from parental control, the fear of burning in a lake of fire and brimstone haunted me like a ghost.

In retrospect, I realize that this fear worked to my advantage. It was a real deterrent to the temptations that surrounded me: illicit drugs, sex, and wild parties, to name a few. However, once I graduated, moved to the big city (Los Angeles), and started a life on my own, I faced a host of debilitating fears. These fears were an *enemy* to my quality of life: fear of flying to my corporate assignments, fear of living in an apartment all alone, fear that every man I met was a wolf in sheep's clothing, fear that any day a major earthquake would swallow up Los Angeles, fear of crossing over a tall bridge. On and on went the torment.

Let me hasten to say that fear is not always a bad thing. Fear is a natural response to real or perceived danger. Healthy fear causes us to lock our car doors, buy alarm systems, and look both ways before crossing the street. Fear becomes unhealthy, however, when it controls our behavior and keeps us from doing positive things. Fear is learned behavior. We can learn it from childhood conditioning, personal experience, observation of other people's experience, media exposure, or other channels of information. Over the years, my apprehensions and trepidations learned through all these channels have been persistent; however, I have been equally persistent in my quest to overcome them.

Although I will generally use the term *fears* throughout the book, not all fears are created equally. Rather, they come in various degrees of intensity: *anxieties, fears,* and *phobias.* Let me explain the differences. *Anxiety* is the dread of a potential danger or loss in the *future* (e.g., possible terrorist attack); *fear* is the emotional response to a real or perceived *present* danger or threat (e.g., being followed); and a *phobia* is a fear gone wild. It is an irrational dread (e.g., fear of elevators) that seeks to avoid repeating a negative experience.

I've modeled the pattern. I saw my fear of earth-quakes progress from *anxiety* about the predicted "big one," to extreme *fear* during a significant temblor, to *quake-phobia* in which I kept an overnight bag packed by the door. Further, until recently, I flatly refused to visit San Francisco under any circumstance due to its devas-tating quakes. It's no wonder that Paul admonished, "Be anxious for nothing, but in everything by prayer and supplication, with thanksgiving, let your requests be made known to God" (Philippians 4:6). He knew that if we didn't nip *anxiety* in the bud, it would progress in its intensity and get a stronghold on our lives.

Whether an anxiety, fear, or phobia, Scripture declares that fear is not from God. "For God has not given us a spirit of fear, but of power and of love and of a sound mind" (2 Timothy 1:7). As a woman of faith, I believe this and I passionately teach it. I also know that "believing is behaving." Therefore, in the final analysis, our *behavior* is the decisive test of what we really believe. When we succumb to the "spirit of fear," it is because we have embraced an erroneous belief about God and His ability or willingness to deliver us from the fear-triggering situation, person, or thing.

I have concluded that I will probably always have to battle one fear or another; however, I have resolved that I will not allow any of them to hinder my progress or derail my destiny. It was Mark Twain who remarked, "Courage is resistance to fear, mastery of fear—not absence of fear."

My goal over the next thirty chapters is to show you how to master thirty common fears. To facilitate our journey, I have grouped these fears into four categories: health and safety fears, relational fears, emotional fears, and financial fears. However, as I contemplated all thirty, I found each to be rooted in one or more of only five core fears:

- fear of pain/death

- fear of inadequacy

- fear of loneliness

- fear of losing control/helplessness

- fear of lack

All fears are a manifestation and often a combination of these core fears. For example, the fear of aging is rooted in the fear of losing control of one's independence, the fear of being left alone, and for many, the fear of a lack of income to maintain a desired lifestyle. We will investigate possible root causes as we discuss each fear.

The solution to overcoming each of the fears involves the same basic approach: *analysis* and *action*. Therefore, I will put each fear in perspective by attempting to give insight and understanding of it through knowledge and education. I will also recommend practical steps to tame it and keep it from controlling you.

I am not a psychologist, hypnotist, or mental health professional. I simply put forth a practical approach to the issues of life based on biblical principles. I do not promise instant deliverance from your fears. I do believe, however, that if by faith in the Word of God, you

implement the recommended strategies, you will experience peace instead of fear. This understanding is crucial
to getting the most out of this book.

Now let's conquer those fears!

Part 1

Health and Safety Fears

Day 1

Fear of Dying

*LORD, remind me how brief
my time on earth will be.
Remind me that my days are numbered—
how fleeting my life is.*

PSALM 39:4 NLT

My father passed away in July 2009 of congestive heart failure. I spent his final month with him in a small, hot town in Texas. Although he'd achieved only an eighth-grade education, he was a successful entrepreneur. Many of the locals held him in high esteem as he cruised the pot-holed streets in his exotic cars. He was very active in his church and enjoyed his status as the top donor. What I found most interesting during the entire ordeal of his impending death was the nature of his final requests:

- "I'd like to hear my sister Althea's voice. Do you think you can arrange that?" She lived on the East Coast and they rarely spoke. There was no rift in the relationship; just never enough time to connect.

- "Tell my sons to come and see about me. I can't take care of myself." All six lived in California and were already en route. He was never the type to express any kind of vulnerability or to do "mushy stuff" like send a birthday card or say, "I love you." I marveled at the power of death to humble the proudest of souls.

I knew that my father was afraid to die, even though he had heard many sermons on death during almost a lifetime in church. Indeed, he had a reason to be afraid, for there was unfinished business between him and a couple of his fellow church leaders. He had flatly refused to forgive them for an offense that had hurt him deeply and had cost him a cherished fifty-year friendship. Of course, he was not without fault in the matter. We'd had many discussions about the situation during the past year. I was more concerned about his unforgiveness than his dying because I knew it was hindering his fellowship with God. Jesus was emphatic about the impact of unforgiveness: "If you do not forgive men their trespasses, neither will your Father forgive your trespasses" (Matthew 6:15).

I finally took matters into my own hands and called his offenders. They expressed a willingness to forgive and finally made the necessary phone calls to reconcile with him. I rejoiced. I also led my father in a prayer of repentance for all his sins. I know that he is now resting in peace.

Fear Analysis

Fear of dying is one of the fundamental or core fears from which many other fears stem, such as fear of doctors, flying, and others that we will discuss later. Every member of the human race will eventually have a date with death. It is inevitable and its timing uncertain; consequently, almost everyone has some modicum of anxiety about it.

When discussing death, it is important to understand that we are eternal beings. Thus, when the Bible speaks of death, it refers to the physical separation of the soul from the body (James 2:26) versus total annihilation. The soul will live eternally in the presence of God or in hell. (Read Luke 16:19-31 for a vivid portrayal of the difference in the quality of the afterlife of Lazarus the beggar compared to the rich man who had ignored Lazarus's daily plea for help.) The decisions that we make during the crucial interval called "time" will determine the *place* and *quality* of our eternal existence. God will make the final call. Thus, many people are afraid to die because of the fear of this final judgment.

Action Plan

American author and humorist Mark Twain once said, "A man who lives fully is prepared to die at any time." This reminds me of a story I heard about an aging church janitor. One night after a passionate sermon on the hereafter, the country pastor asked the small congregation, "How many of you want to go to heaven?" All raised their hands except old Jim, who sat quietly in the back still clad in his work uniform. The pastor, puzzled at his response, said, "Jim, don't you want to go to heaven?"

"Yup," came his reply.

"Well, why didn't you raise your hand?"

"Thought you were trying to get up a load for tonight!"

Like Jim, we all want to go to heaven, but not tonight. Let's look at what we can do now to conquer the fear of dying:

- *Prepare for death spiritually and emotionally.* We prepare spiritually by accepting Jesus as our Lord and Savior and living a life of obedience to His Word by the power of God. Emotionally, we must accept the inevitability of death—especially when death is imminent.

Elizabeth Kübler-Ross, a pioneer in the study of the effects of death and dying, explained that most of us go through the following stages as we face our death:

1. Shock Stage: "Oh, my God!"

2. Denial Stage: "It can't be true!"

3. Anger Stage: "Why me?"

4. Bargaining Stage: "Spare me, God, and I will do something for You."

5. Depression Stage: "It's all over. I have nothing to look forward to."

6. Testing Stage: "What can I do to make my remaining days worthwhile?"

7. Acceptance Stage: "It doesn't make sense to fight the inevitable."[1]

Only the grace of God can empower us to experience inexplicable peace as we accept our Divine destiny.

- *Prepare relationally.* We need to let the key people in our lives know how much we care about them. We must also forgive everyone who has hurt or offended us. This is critical to getting our own sins forgiven. We must also ask forgiveness from others for our trespasses against them.

- *Prepare financially.* Being financially unprepared is surely a cause for legitimate concern—especially if you have dependents. Be smart and, at a minimum, get burial insurance and prepare a will that spells out who will handle your affairs and who will inherit specific assets. A will can be handwritten and notarized. As a certified public accountant, I recommend you not only have a will (for special, sentimental assets), but a *living trust* (for real estate, investments) and an *advanced directive* that sets forth your preferences regarding the use of possible life-extending measures.

- *Submit to His sovereignty.* Neutralizing the fear of death requires focusing on living life to the fullest. My concern when contemplating my own demise has always centered on *how* I will make that transition. I don't wish to die violently nor do I want to suffer a protracted illness. (I'm hoping for an "Enoch deal" [Genesis 5:24] where God just takes me up!) Meanwhile, since I have no control over how I'm going to die, I have decided just to let my "requests be made known to God" (Philippians 4:6-7) and to submit to His sovereignty. When the time comes, He will be there to give me the grace I need to join Him for a life of eternal bliss.

What reason can you give for why you would be afraid to die—tonight? Have you lived a life of selfishness and disobedience, and thus fear eternal damnation? Or can you confidently say, "I have fought the good fight, I have finished the race, I have kept the faith" (2 Timothy 4:7)? If not, what must you do now to be ready to make that eternal transition? Do you need to forgive an offense, express your affection, or apologize for your wrongdoings? If an angelic messenger were to show up and announce, "Tonight's the night!" know that death ushers believers into the presence of the Lord where there is fullness of joy.

Day 2

Fear of Doctors and Needles

"Fear is that little darkroom where
negatives are developed."
MICHAEL PRITCHARD, YOUTH ACTIVIST

Vera's adrenaline went into overdrive when she felt a pea-sized lump in her breast during her morning shower. Her twenty-year-old daughter urged her to see a doctor right away, but Vera was too petrified. She, like so many other women, didn't actually fear the doctor; she feared his diagnosis—cancer. She was only forty-eight years old. The year was 1973 and the medical advances that have greatly reduced the number of deaths from breast cancer were yet to be developed. Thus, most women considered breast cancer a sure death sentence. Vera was steadfast in refusing to see a doctor—until the lump grew to the size of a small egg. By then, it was too late. The cancer had metastasized to other parts of her body, and she died within eighteen months. Her daughter was torn between grief and anger at what she termed an "unnecessary early death."

Vera was not alone in her fear of medical professionals.

Some people are so blinded by their fear of dentists, they neglect regular dental checkups. Dr. William Nordquist, named the 2008 International Dentist of the Year by the American Academy of Implant Dentistry, asserts that any bacteria in the mouth with resulting chronic infection (including periodontal disease) may potentially lead to heart disease.[2] Heart disease is the number one killer of women, claiming over 500,000 lives annually. Untreated tooth infections have indeed led to death. On February 28, 2007, the *Washington Post* reported the story of twelve-year-old Deamonte Driver who died after an infection from a tooth abscess spread to his brain. A routine tooth extraction might have saved him.

Fear does not have a gender bias. Untold numbers of men have died from prostate cancer. Most would have survived had the cancer been detected in an earlier stage. Some were too fearful to see a doctor. They put on their "macho masks" and buried their heads in the sand—only to suffer the consequence. Also tragic is the number of folks who would gladly see a doctor if they could be assured that they would never have to encounter a needle.

Fear Analysis

Fearing the doctor is rooted in the core fear of pain or death. Of course, many people who fear doctors have experienced a traumatic event at some point in their lives and have resolved never to relive the emotional and physical pain. Well, friend, doctors are God's assistants on earth and a vital part of His service team. In His sovereignty, He often chooses to cure our diseases and infirmities through medicine as opposed to a miracle. To guard against putting more faith in doctors than the Great Physician, I constantly remind myself that God created my body, and He alone determines whether any treatment or medications will be effective. He is in complete control of the outcome.

If you have assumed that embracing the medical profession is an indication of weak faith, it's time for some mental reprogramming. Luke, described by the apostle Paul as "the beloved physician" (see Colossians 4:14), was the writer of the Gospel of Luke and the Book of Acts. He was one of the spiritual leaders in the early church. Thus, there is no rationale for equating doctors with lack of spirituality. It's time to cast down those imaginations that can keep you from the prevention and early detection of diseases. Do not allow your core fear of dying to become a self-fulfilling prophecy in which your avoidance of doctors ultimately leads to your death!

Action Plan

To overcome your fear of doctors or needles, educate yourself on why you *need* to get various exams and checkups. Further, empower yourself by researching the background, causes, statistics, and stories of any condition that you know (or suspect) you may have in order to find the latest developments in treating it. Simply go to www.google.com (or any Internet search engine) and type in the name of the suspected disorder.

Here are other tips that will prove helpful:

- Surround yourself with people of faith (prayer and Bible study group) who have a balanced view of God and will encourage you to take practical steps to getting help while standing in faith for supernatural healing.

- Don't assume that you are a victim of any disease simply because you may have one or two symptoms of it. Instead, make a note to inform the doctor about them during your visit.

- Develop a list of questions to ask the doctor. Don't depend on your memory since you may already be fraught with anxiety about seeing him.

- Don't assume the doctor's time is more valuable than yours. Let him know you have some anxiety about the visit and would like him to answer questions to put you at ease. Know that the doctor is there to help you.

- If you must get a shot but dread the pain of the needle prick, be sure to tell the medical staff about your experience in getting shots. I always inform them that I have small rolling veins and get better results with a butterfly or infant needle. I also ask for the best phlebotomist available to draw the blood. Further, I remind myself that the pain of a needle prick or the impact of the injected medication lasts only a few seconds.

- When getting ready for a dental treatment, develop a plan with the doctor on how you'll signal him to stop if the pain gets too intense. If he's insensitive or impatient, find another doctor. Caution! Don't be too quick to switch; the consistency of seeing the same doctor should make you more at ease since he will be familiar with your history. Just ask him to be more gentle.

- Get to know your doctor personally by asking him about his training or other not-so-personal matters. This establishes rapport and minimizes the feeling of talking to a stranger.

- Consider how effective you are going to be in pursuing your destiny without the limitations of a malfunctioning body.

Day 3

Fear of Becoming Disabled

*"There are so many opportunities in life,
that the loss of two or three capabilities
is not necessarily debilitating."*
JIM DAVIS, AMERICAN CARTOONIST
AND CREATOR OF GARFIELD

At the tender age of seventeen, Joni Eareckson Tada dove headlong into shallow water. The resulting injury left her a quadriplegic. During her two years of rehabilitation, she learned how to paint beautiful, marketable artwork by holding a brush between her teeth. She also went on to write many bestselling books and to establish several award-winning programs that meet the needs of disabled people around the world. Several honorary doctorate degrees and a movie about her life attest to the impact of her work.

I got a taste of what it would be like to have a long-term disability when a severe case of sciatica sent me to the hospital for four days in early 2010. I was totally incapacitated when I came home. Being unable to engage in my regular routine of preparing meals, bathing myself, getting to the restroom without assistance, and other conveniences seemed surreal. I believe with all my heart "that all things work together for good to those who love God, to those who are the called according to His purpose" (Romans 8:28)—even if I never comprehend what the "good" is. Therefore, I never asked, "Why me?" I refused to entertain any thoughts that my condition might be permanent. Many prayed for my healing. By the grace of God, I had a miraculous recovery. Within six weeks, I fulfilled a speaking engagement in Montreal, Canada and afterward shopped the streets of the fashion district—on foot!

Fear Analysis

During most stages of your life, your risk of becoming disabled is higher than your risk of dying. Studies show that three out of ten Americans entering the work force today will become disabled before they retire.[3] The fear of becoming disabled is rooted in at least three core fears: fear of loneliness, fear of inadequacy, and fear of lack. We see aloneness demonstrated in the story of the paralytic who lay at the pool of Bethesda with a thirty-eight-year disability (John 5:1-15). He explained to Jesus that he had no one to put him in the water when the angel came and stirred it. Where were his family and friends? It is tragic to have no support base. Fortunately, Jesus healed him.

Many fear disablement because they think others would perceive them as "less than" or inadequate to continue their normal role. I've even noticed at social functions how some treat wheelchair-bound people as if they were invisible. The masses won't engage them in conversation or, if they do, their tone may be overly sympathetic—which is even more humiliating to the disabled person.

Thomas Edison, famed inventor, pioneer in harnessing the benefits of electricity, and founder of General Electric, one of the largest corporations in the world, had a learning disability. His mother began home schooling him at age seven to spare him the humiliation she observed from his teacher. At age thirteen, he caught scarlet fever, from which he became almost deaf. This handicap strongly influenced his behavior, his career, the focus of his work, and desire to improve humanity. It motivated him to develop over a thousand inventions, including the phonograph.

Perhaps the biggest concern of disablement is financial lack. The beggar in Acts 3 who was lame from birth is a vivid reminder of what it's like to be poor and disabled. Fortunately, he appeared to have a good support system for "they" laid him "daily at the gate of the temple, which is called Beautiful, to ask alms from those who entered the temple" (Acts 3:2). After he encountered Peter and John, who offered healing rather than money, his begging days were over.

Action Plan

A disability is not a death sentence and overcoming the fear of it is possible with the right mindset. Try these practical strategies:

- Be grateful for each day that you enjoy physical wholeness; consider it a gift from God and not an entitlement.

- Be vigilant in maintaining good health through proper diet and exercise. Freak accidents like Joni's are not the usual cause of long-term disabilities. Rather, cancer, heart disease, back injuries, and other illnesses are the culprits.

- Sow seeds of service into the lives of others (neighbors, young people, relatives). Who knows when you'll need to reap a kindness?

- Minimize your financial fears of becoming disabled by purchasing long-term disability insurance. The ideal policy covers at least 60 percent of your income, has a waiting period shorter than your savings can last, and pays benefits until you reach retirement age. The average long-term disability lasts two and a half years. You'll want to seek financial counseling on how much insurance you'll need. Know that it is not cheap!

- Believe it is God's desire for you to "prosper in all things and be in health, just as your soul prospers" (3 John 2).

Joni refused to see her disabled body as a prison. She persevered and turned her lemon into lemonade. Here is what she says she'll tell Jesus when she meets Him face to face: "The weaker I felt in this chair, the harder I leaned on You. And the harder I leaned, the more I discovered how strong You are. Thank You, Jesus, for learning obedience in Your suffering…You gave me grace to learn obedience in mine."

Day 4

Fear of Creepy, Crawly Things

*Thou hast created all things, and for thy
pleasure they are and were created.*
REVELATION 4:11 KJV

You may find it hard to fathom that *everything* God created—even snakes, spiders, and rodents—was for His pleasure. The very thought of these crawlies makes most people (including me!) shudder. The most feared of these is the snake. This forked-tongued creature that originally talked and walked, has been associated with evil ever since he eased into the Garden of Eden, called God a liar, and tricked Adam and Eve into eating the forbidden fruit from the Tree of the Knowledge of Good and Evil (Genesis 3:1-19). God's judgment of the serpent was swift and severe. He banished him to a life of slithering on the ground and having a mutually antagonistic relationship with humans.

Fear Analysis

The fear of creepy, crawly things is rooted in the fear of pain or even death. It is indeed wise to have a healthy fear or deep respect for the life-threatening dangers and discomfort crawlies can bring. Otherwise, we would not respond wisely and quickly in the presence of real danger.

An unhealthy fear of crawlies, however, may sometimes be the result of their negative portrayal in movies and the media and not from our personal experiences. Why, even the macho movie character Indiana Jones had a fear of snakes!

But really, how many direct encounters have you had with a snake? And when was the last time you resisted a black widow or the venomous brown recluse spider? Has a rodent bitten you or transmitted a disease to you? Probably not.

But if you have had a bad experience, there is still hope for overcoming any related phobias. We tend to fear what we do not understand. Therefore, knowledge is a key factor in overcoming fear of crawlies. Perhaps the following observations will help you develop a better appreciation for why they are on the planet and may help mitigate your fear and loathing of them.

Snakes are very important to our environment. They do not pursue humans for food nor seek to attack them— except in Hollywood movies. They merely respond aggressively when they perceive a threat. They serve as natural pest controllers by feeding on rodents, which often carry diseases. Their presence reduces the need for rodent-ridding chemicals that can be harmful to animal and plant life, which saves farmers lots of money. The snake is prominent in the symbol for the American medical profession and for good reason. Snake venom research has led to the development of several life-saving and pain-relieving drugs that treat conditions ranging from rheumatoid arthritis to heart attacks.

Spiders keep cockroaches and flies at bay in your home. In agricultural fields, they show up in abundance and minimize the effect of destructive insects, saving billions annually. In addition to reducing local disease-carrying insects, spiders provide humans with other medical benefits. Spider venom is used in neurological research and may prevent permanent brain damage in stroke victims. The silk produced by spiders is used in many optical devices, including laboratory instruments.[4]

Rodents, as laboratory test subjects, have led to the discovery of treatments and cures for many human disorders. Laboratory mice are widely considered to be the best model of inherited human disease and share 99 percent of their genes with humans. Mice and humans share similarities in nervous, cardiovascular, endocrine, immune, musculoskeletal, and other internal organ systems.[5] Mice are also ideal because of their size, low cost, ease of handling, and fast reproduction rate.

Action Plan

- Get educated about the crawlies you despise. Visit a zoo or a pet store to get an up-close view of them. Even if they are caged, you'll get a better perspective than you'll get from the media. Ask about their habits and unique traits.

- Take steps to reduce your likelihood of encountering a crawly. For example, snakes like to hide under firewood and heavy foliage. Therefore, I always tap a planter or stack of wood before I move them; it's my way of "knocking," alerting crawlies to my presence. When getting dressed, shake out your purse or shoes that you haven't worn for a while; a spider may have found refuge there. Just being aware of their preferred hangouts is empowering.

- If you have observed an inordinate number of spiders or rodents in or around your home, consider having them exterminated.

- Rest on the Lord's promise: "Behold, I give you the authority to trample on serpents and scorpions, and over all the power of the enemy, and nothing shall by any means hurt you" (Luke 10:19).

Remember, your goal is not to become chummy with crawlies but to not allow them to sabotage your peace or to affect your quality of life, such as never sitting in your backyard or never again entering the attic, which holds a lifetime of memories, simply because you saw a mouse last time you were there.

Day 5

Fear of Dogs

*"The average dog is a nicer person
than the average person."*
ANDREW (ANDY) ROONEY,
AMERICAN RADIO AND TV WRITER

Jane believes she has finally met Mr. Right. They are compatible in almost every aspect of their relationship—except one. Jane has a morbid fear of dogs; Mr. Right is the proud owner of two American pit bull terriers.

This notorious breed is responsible for the most human deaths of any other dog in America, but pit bulls are not inherently vicious or dangerous. In fact, they are stable, intelligent, and highly trainable. In conjunction with local law enforcement, they play an important role in their community by locating missing people. In their off-duty hours, they do charity work as therapy dogs. Petey, the faithful dog on the long-running TV show *The Little Rascals*, was a pit bull. He spent countless hours with children day after day and never hurt anyone. The pit bull has earned a bad reputation because some mean people have abused their dogs and trained them to be aggressive.[6]

But unless Jane takes steps to overcome her fear of dogs, no wedding bells will be ringing for her in the near future.

Fear Analysis

The fear of dogs is rooted in the core fear of pain or death. It is indeed a rational fear since some dogs are trained to be aggressive, and news reports of actual deaths from dog attacks are not uncommon. If a dog has ever chased, growled, or snarled at you, there's a good chance you may still experience some anxiety when you encounter one. If you have been attacked or bitten by a canine, or know or heard of someone who was, you most likely avoid dogs at all costs.

Dogs make wonderful pets. How can we ever forget the heartwarming stories and feats of the sensitive, intelligent, and protective collie that starred in the television series *Lassie*? She was truly a man's best friend. Of course, dogs have exhibited behavior on both ends of the scale—even the dogs in the Bible. Dogs literally consumed the body of the wicked queen Jezebel, leaving only her skull, hands, and feet (2 Kings 9:30-37), but they compassionately licked the sores of Lazarus the beggar (Luke 16:21). (By the way, studies show a dog's saliva contains antibacterial substances and healing properties.)

In certain circumstances, any type of dog can be dangerous; even an otherwise docile dog can inflict great harm in the wrong circumstance.

Action Plan

- Stop confessing that you are afraid of dogs. Faith comes by hearing, so you need to hear yourself say, "I am peaceful around dogs."

- Recall and evaluate the circumstance or event that caused you to start fearing dogs. Chances are it was a one-time occurrence. If so, why do you live in constant expectation of a repeat episode?

- Engage dog-walkers in brief conversations about the breed of their dog and his habits. Be genuinely curious. Caution! It's not a good idea to pet a strange dog. Always get the owner's permission first.

- Pet a friend's puppy and engage with him frequently as he grows.

- Visit a dog park and, from a comfortable distance (perhaps from your parked car), observe the demeanor of the various dogs. Imagine how much fun you too could have with such an accepting friend that loves unconditionally.

- When you see an approaching dog, breathe deeply, stay calm, and say to yourself, *This is somebody's friend and companion. He is not out to get me.* The fact that you can see his teeth is not a sign that he wants to bite you!

- If you walk or bike in areas prone to dogs, always be prepared to defend yourself with a sturdy stick, lightweight pipe, or other tool. "A prudent person foresees danger and takes precautions. The simpleton goes blindly on and suffers the consequences" (Proverbs 22:3 NLT). You never know when you're encountering a dog trained to be aggressive toward humans.

- Heed conventional dog trainers' wisdom if you are ever confronted by a dog. Generally, they advise: (1) Do not run. Dogs love a chase, and you cannot outrun them. (2) Stand still and keep your hands in your pockets. Dogs often see hands as moving targets to latch onto. (3) Firmly yell a command, such as "Go!" or "Get home!"(4) Bend down as if to pick up a rock; dogs know what this body language means and will usually back off at the threat of pain. (Hey, they have fears too!) Many trainers advise against looking dogs in the eyes as some dogs perceive this to be an act of confrontation. Rather, turn to the side and firmly shout a phrase similar to the ones mentioned in point (3).

- Develop an appreciation for dogs' value to society. Read news stories of their heroic acts. Especially moving are the accounts of military dogs deployed in war zones. They assist

in finding bombs and lost soldiers, and they
save lives and boost morale among troops.

I realize that some of the information and advice
above will be useless when you round the corner and
find yourself face-to-face with a Doberman pinscher!
Just remember that Divine protection is not limited by
the size of the threat.

It wasn't until I started writing this book that I
decided it was time to stop panicking or running the
other way when I encountered a dog. I reviewed online
photos of the most vicious dog breeds as well as the
friendliest. I asked the Holy Spirit for grace to pet certain dogs and to just relax in the presence of others. And
I am holding fast to the Word of God: "I sought the
Lord, and He heard me, and delivered me from all my
fears" (Psalm 34:4).

Remember, your goal is not to become sociable with
every dog you meet but to experience peace rather than
fear in their presence.

Day 6

Fear of Enclosed Spaces

*"He who fears something gives
it power over him."*
MOORISH PROVERB

On a recent road trip to Utah, I was having the time of my life enjoying the majestic views of Zion National Park—until we approached the mile-long Zion–Mt. Carmel Tunnel. I hate tunnels. I resisted the urge to suggest to my husband and friends that we simply turn around since we were just sightseeing with no particular destination in mind. To boot, we would have to return to our hotel using the same route, which meant another trip back through the tunnel. Determined not to allow fear and anxiety to dictate my behavior and the quality of my life, I took a deep breath and cast down the thought of suffocating in the tunnel should an earthquake cause it to collapse while we were inside. Of course, we survived the round-trip without incident, and I racked up another triumph over fear. Again, that's what this book on taming fears is all about—learning to move from fear to peace by exercising faith.

Fear Analysis

Claustrophobia, the fear of small or enclosed spaces, is one of the most common phobias. It is rooted in the core fear of *losing control* and in some instances, *fear of dying*. As with most phobias, claustrophobia begins with a traumatic incident usually suffered as a child, such as being locked or trapped in a closet or other small space. For others, such as my friend Dee, claustrophobia develops later in life from traumatic experiences like being stuck in an elevator. To this day, she panics at the thought of taking an elevator and makes every effort to avoid them.

People with claustrophobia can also struggle with closets, caves, tunnels, MRI machines, airplanes, and congested traffic. Some feel anxious when people violate their personal space by standing too closely. Other sufferers get panicky even wearing restrictive clothing. The tendency to avoid these panic triggers can have a crippling effect on a claustrophobe's life. Further, their urge to flee the situation can keep them from being rational and calm enough to cast down their debilitating thoughts. Consider these examples of avoidance behaviors:

- Sue hates sitting underneath a balcony in a theater. Rather than enjoying the presentation, she is constantly thinking of her escape route.

- When Betty travels, she insists on a hotel room on the lowest possible floor so she can minimize the length of time she must be on the elevator. She often takes the stairs, putting herself in even more danger from possible assault.

- Because of Tom's continued back pain, his doctor recommended an MRI of his spine. Tom gets panicky even at the thought of an open MRI machine, so he continues to delay scheduling the critical exam.

- Frank loves socializing, but he always stands near the door at a party so he can be the first one out should the room have to be evacuated.

In each of these cases, the avoidance reinforces the fear and can force the sufferer into isolation and depression.

Action Plan

If you suffer from claustrophobia, here's what you need to do to get your life back:

- Make a commitment to yourself to stop avoiding the fear-triggering situation.

- Find a nonclaustrophobic "deliverance partner" who can accompany, encourage, and pray for you as you set specific times to face your giant. For example, if you plan to overcome a fear of elevators, set a date to visit at least a ten-story building. Make several trips on the elevator; make the final one without your partner. You may have to progress more gradually depending on the severity of your fear.

• Remember that any building with an elevator has likely passed certain safety standards, and those who manage the building are usually prepared to handle whatever goes wrong. Your safety is in their best interests.

• When you encounter an enclosed situation, ignore your increased heartbeat, perspiration, light-headedness, shaking, or other symptoms. Know that fear dies hard. Breathe deeply to slow the adrenaline rush. This will allow you to think more clearly. Focus on relaxation. Remember that the opposite of fear is peace. Declare inwardly, *I am letting the peace of God rule in my heart right now* (Colossians 3:15).

• As you approach the enclosed space, make a Scripture-based faith declaration, such as: *God is with me in this situation for He will never leave me nor forsake me* (Hebrews 13:5). Or, *Because I have made God my refuge, He has commanded His angels to guard me in all my ways* (Psalms 91:10-11). Use your God-given imagination to visualize yourself surrounded with angels mandated to protect you.

Day 7

Fear of Heights

Praise the LORD from the heavens;
praise Him in the heights!
PSALM 148:1

The glass elevator at the 1815-foot Canadian National (CN) Tower ascended rapidly to the 114th-floor observation deck—but not as rapidly as my heart rate. I was determined, however, not to let my anxiety about heights deprive me of touring the tallest freestanding structure in the Americas and the second tallest in the world (surpassed only by the 2717-foot Burj Khalifa complex in Dubai, United Arab Emirates). I would surely brag about my bravery later.

Toronto is a beautiful city and the CN Tower attracts millions of visitors each year. Its award-winning revolving restaurant provides a magnificent view of the city. However, the fact that I could see the roof of every single skyscraper did not escape my observation and was a little unnerving. I also had to cast down thoughts such as, *What if terrorists were to bomb the structure while we're inside?* and *What if there's an earthquake?* I had already done my research and knew that Toronto was prone to quakes.

As I've learned to do, I replaced my fearful musing with the question Jesus asked His disciples during one of their anxious moments: "Why are you so fearful? How is it that you have no faith?" (Mark 4:40). Since this was the highest altitude I'd ever ascended outside of an airplane, it was a defining moment in overcoming my fear of heights.

I revisited the CN Tower with an adventurous friend two years later. Admittedly, I was still a little squeamish about the glass-elevator ride, but it is amazing how taming a fear gives you a new perspective. A year after that, as I entered the elevator at the Empire State Building in New York City en route to the 86th-floor observation deck, I felt like an old pro. Yes, I had a fleeting thought about a terrorist attack, but I quickly reminded myself that I am never away from God's protecting presence.

My fear of heights is now under subjection to the Holy Spirit; it is not dictating or deterring my actions. Dubai, here I come!

Fear Analysis

Acrophobia, the fear of heights, is rooted in the core fears of *pain and death* and *helplessness or losing control*. It is one of the most common fears and holds millions hostage. Of course, there is a reason or foundation for every fear. If you are afraid of heights, at some point in your life you probably experienced a traumatic event involving height or saw someone else do so. The degree of your acrophobia usually is determined by how traumatic the event was that triggered the phobia. Understanding why you have a certain fear is often a good place to start in overcoming it.

When I was a child, a rickety bridge collapsed over a creek as we attempted to cross in the family car. It was nighttime to boot. It seemed like an eternity before someone came along the rural road and, with great effort, pulled us out with chains. We were never in danger of drowning as the water was only a few feet high; however, to this day I think about that incident whenever I cross a bridge—not with extreme fear but with moderate trepidation.

A fear of heights can disrupt people's lives in subtle ways. Some may refuse to put up holiday lights outside their house because of the need to use a ladder. Others may decline a promising job offer because the office is located in a skyscraper or dismiss even a virtual helicopter sightseeing tour.

Action Plan

Starting today, you can take steps to help yourself overcome acrophobia.

- Envision at least two things you would do and the fun you could have if you were not bound by acrophobia. Let the prospect of doing them become your motivation.

- Plan to overcome the fear in small steps by gradually exposing yourself to the *least* fearful situation and moving to the *most* fearful. For example, in a multilevel parking structure, you could take the stairs and look over the edge at the top of each floor. No need to go all the way to the top on the first try.

- As you face the fear, control your physical symptoms of rapid heartbeat and nervousness by breathing deeply and consciously relaxing your stomach and shoulder muscles. This will help you to continue to think rationally; otherwise, you may panic and give up the pursuit.

- Confront acrophobia with a brave and adventurous friend who will encourage your faith and discourage your fear along the way. Avoid those who tell you to just "get over it!" Seek those who can respect your fear but guide you toward deliverance.

- Put the fear in perspective. Consider how often your worst fear has actually happened. Really now, how often has the skyscraper, the ladder, or the bridge collapsed over the past ten or twenty years, if ever?

You may never become an Alain Robert,[7] who has successfully climbed over eighty skyscrapers with his bare hands, but with patience, perseverance, and support, you can overcome fear of heights.

Day 8

Fear of Flying

Your love, LORD, reaches to the heavens,
your faithfulness to the skies.
PSALM 36:5 NIV

"If God wanted me to fly, He would have given me wings!" my eighty-eight-year-old Aunt Creola adamantly declares. Her fear of flying is well-known. Notwithstanding, she demonstrated surprising bravery recently and flew from Dallas to Los Angeles for my milestone birthday celebration. Shortly after she returned home, she was working in her yard when she heard the sound of a plane overhead. When she looked up, she suddenly realized how high above the clouds she had actually flown. Her old fear returned with a vengeance.

She is not alone. Millions of people are anxious about flying. And since the September 11, 2001 attack on the World Trade Center, their concerns have expanded beyond turbulence, mechanical failures, or pilot error and now center on the threat of terrorist violence.

I confess that although I have boarded many a flight, I have never been totally at ease about flying. But I decided in 1994, before embarking upon a twenty-three hour flight to South Africa, that fear was not going to keep me from exploring the world and enjoying the awesome beauty of God's creation.

Fear Analysis

Aerophobia, fear of flying, is rooted in the core fears of *pain and death* and *helplessness or losing control*. However, it is often an indirect combination of other phobias, such as the fear of enclosed spaces or a fear of heights.

Now, reminding you that flying is actually safer than riding in a car may not help you much, but the reality is that your chances of being involved in an aircraft accident are about one in eleven million. Your chances of being killed in an automobile accident are one in five thousand.[8]

For most people who hate flying, turbulence is the biggest anxiety-producer. Captain Keith Godfrey, former British Airways pilot, explains: "Turbulence is the irregular movement of the air. When air travels across the ground it hits things like buildings, towns, hills, and mountains and causes the air to bob up and down." He further declares that turbulence is not dangerous (if you stay buckled in your seat) and cannot bring a plane out of the sky.[9] My brother holds a key position with a major aircraft manufacturer. He confirms that the wings on an average commercial plane can flex over thirty feet up or down and still be safe aerodynamically and structurally.

Action Plan

- Gain a basic understanding of how safe it is to travel, how planes work, and other aspects of air travel. A simple Google search will produce some wonderful sites such as www.Flying withoutfear.com, www.TravelDirt.com, www .FearofFlyingHelp.com, and others loaded with free information ranging from takeoff sounds to landing basics.

- By faith, picture yourself calm, cool, and collected especially during takeoff and landing. I often take my pulse on takeoff and dare it to change!

- When booking your ticket, consider selecting a seat over the wing of the plane. This area is more stable and you'll feel less impact from any turbulence. The website www.seatguru .com allows you to view the layout of your plane prior to booking. You'll need to know the aircraft that will be used for your flight before going to the site, and you can usually find this information on the airline's website.

- Be sure to pack a good book or magazine, music, or whatever distractions amuse you. I often put the praise and worship music on my iPod on blast. By the time I finish hearing songs that exalt God and His power, the fear of flying fades away.

- Engage your travel mates in conversation—about anything. Talking with others will make you feel more relaxed and keep your mind from focusing on the fact that you are thirty-seven thousand feet off the ground.

- Breathe deeply through tense, turbulent moments. Inhale through your nose for ten seconds, exhale with your mouth slightly open for ten seconds. This will lower your heart rate by slowing the flow of adrenaline.

- Know that you are in experienced hands since a commercial airline pilot must complete extensive training and log thousands of flight hours to become a captain. Besides, Captain Jesus is always onboard and crises are His specialty.

- Since faith is the bridge from fear to peace, get into faith mode by memorizing, meditating on, and reciting (or even printing out) Psalm 108:4. Make it your declaration: "For great is your love, higher than the heavens; your faithfulness reaches to the skies" (NIV).

Yes, God will be faithful to His promise to be with you always—even in the skies.

Day 9

Fear of Drowning

*"Do the thing you fear and the
death of fear is certain."*
RALPH WALDO EMERSON

"Lord, save us! We're going to drown!" (Matthew 8:25 NLT). The disciples were in a panic. Some of them were fishermen whose chief occupational hazard was drowning. Surely they had experienced tense moments on the water. However, this was no ordinary storm; the waves had already begun to swamp the boat. Meanwhile, Jesus was sound asleep. At their alert, He arose and simply commanded the winds and waves to be still. Once again, they witnessed His great power. "The disciples were amazed. 'Who is this man?' they asked. 'Even the winds and waves obey him!'" (Matthew 8:27 NLT).

Have you ever had a bad experience with water? Have you dismissed the thought of ever taking an ocean cruise for fear of a repeat of the *Titanic*? What about gliding through a gleaming swimming pool or snorkeling in refreshing waters with beautiful marine life at your fingertips? Is the fear of drowning keeping you from enjoying life's fullness? Do you really believe God is Lord over land, air, and water?

I am not a great swimmer, but after at least three *beginning* swimming lessons, I know a few basics. My husband often tells the story of how I lost my balance one day (over thirty years ago) while we were frolicking in a pool. I started flailing my arms and screaming for dear life. Finally, roaring with laughter, he pulled me up. He couldn't imagine why I was so frightened since all I needed to do was stand up. The water was only chest-high! But I feared drowning. Since then, I have limited my swimming to the "below the neck" section of a pool or any body of water—even when snorkeling. My goal over the next year, however, is to get really comfortable in the deep end of the pool. I've already identified the training facility where I'll accomplish my goal.

Fear Analysis

Aquaphobia, the fear of water, is rooted in the core fears of *pain and death* and *helplessness or losing control*. According to a 1998 Gallup poll sponsored by the Miracle Swimming Institute (MSI),[10] 64 percent of adults in the U.S. are fearful in open water, 46 percent are afraid in deep-water pools, and 39 percent are afraid to put their heads under water.[11] Melon Dash, MSI founder, specializes in training fearful people to swim. Such fear of water often leads people to a lifetime of avoidance; however, the consequences go beyond recreational advantage. Individuals may find themselves in the water without knowing how to swim, and their very survival is at stake.

As in most fears surrounding general safety concerns, aquaphobia can usually be traced to a prior unpleasant experience. (There are several specific phobias related to water, but they are beyond the scope of our discussion.) Fearful parents also hand down this fear to their children. Despite the origin of your fear of water, you can overcome it.

Action Plan

One of the keys to overcoming your fear of drowning is to become comfortable and confident in water. Here's what to do:

- A swimming pool is the best controlled environment for a beginner. Therefore, I suggest you enroll in a swim class taught by sensitive, qualified instructors. Consider reading *Conquer Your Fear of Water* by Melon Dash.[12] This book, along with an instructional DVD, is packed with informative and encouraging details that will put you at ease.

- Enlist another person who desires to overcome her fear of drowning to take the swim class with you. "Two people are better off than one, for they can help each other succeed" (Ecclesiastes 4:9).

- Learn how water works. It is by nature buoyant; it will support your body weight and allow you to float no matter how much you weigh. I swore I was the exception to the rule and would go straight to the bottom of the pool. Not so. The key is simply to relax.

- Remind yourself that you are already pre-disposed to succeed in the water due to your body's composition. Up to 60 percent of the human body is water. The brain is composed of 70 percent water, and the lungs are nearly 90 percent water. Lean muscle tissue contains about 75 percent water by weight. Body fat contains 10 percent water and bone has 22 percent water. About 83 percent of our blood is water.[13] Prepare to float big time!

- Whenever you encounter water, acknowledge the presence of God. Breathe deeply and envision the angels surrounding and supporting you.

- Gradually engage in other water-related activities, such as a short cruise or boat ride around a local harbor or lake (versus a two-week Caribbean cruise). No need to fear. Remember that even the winds and the waves obey Him.

Day 10

Fear of Natural Disasters

Though a thousand fall at your side,
though ten thousand are dying around you,
these evils will not touch you.

PSALM 91:7 NLT

Earthquakes. Tornados. Hurricanes. Floods. Volcanic eruptions. The occurrence of these destructive forces of nature is often referred to as an "act of God." Of course, theologians debate whether they are indeed acts of God—that is, divinely initiated rather than just a natural occurrence in a sinful world. Some argue that God *sends* them as an act of judgment; others contend He merely *permits* them to achieve His divine purpose. My thoughts regarding this debate are summed up in Romans 11:33 (NLT): "Oh, how great are God's riches and wisdom and knowledge! How impossible it is for us to understand his decisions and his ways!" God is sovereign—and in control of the universe.

Now, regardless of their underlying causes, the mere thought of a natural disaster can strike fear in the hearts of those who live in disaster-prone areas. I know. I live in Los Angeles—earthquake country. I love this city. It is unsurpassed in its year-round recreational versatility due to the awesome weather. Its breathtaking mountain views, its endless entertainment attractions, and its cultural diversity overshadow the inconvenience of its legendary traffic jams. It's an amazing place, and I'm a loyal citizen—until it starts shaking. Then I'm ready to move far away—to anywhere that doesn't shake!

I've spent way too many hours thinking about earthquakes and allowing the possibility of one to control my behavior. The slightest tremor has often stolen my peace of mind for days. No more. God has done a wonderful work of grace in my heart, and I have tamed the fear (read, *I wisely run for cover when the shaking starts*). I'm not letting it stop me from enjoying life in this great city.

Fear Analysis

The fear of natural disasters is rooted in the core fears of *pain and death*, *helplessness or losing control*, and perhaps even the fear of *lack*, as many never recover financially from the losses they sustain. Natural disasters have been the focus for many blockbuster movies including *Twister*, *Earthquake*, *Volcano*, and *Deep Impact*. The portrayals of the disasters are overwhelmingly horrific. While the goal of the producers was simply to entertain, the anxiety that these films caused has had a lasting impact on many.

Interestingly, natural disasters are not even in the top ten leading causes of death. In the United States, the majority of people die from heart disease, cancer, and strokes. Famine and disease also claim more lives in other parts of the world. Notwithstanding, 2010 was a record year for disaster-related deaths due primarily to the Haiti earthquake, which claimed over 300,000 lives.

Action Plan

Whatever type of natural disaster you may face, preparation is the key to survival physically and financially. Here are some wise moves to make:

- If it's available, purchase as much disaster insurance as your budget will allow. Read the fine print and understand the amount of your deductible in the event of an occurrence (the higher the deductible the lower the premiums). Make every effort to save the amount of the deductible in your emergency reserve fund.

- Conduct emergency preparedness drills at home at least quarterly. Check flashlights and batteries to assure their readiness. We had a blackout recently and discovered that the batteries in our main lantern were corroded. We erroneously thought we were prepared.

- Store at least a three-day supply of water (two weeks is better) for each family member. The American Red Cross recommends one gallon per person per day for consumption and hygiene. Don't forget that your water-heater tank is a source of water if needed—and if accessible.

- Store at least a three-day supply of nonperishable food for each family member. Avoid those with high sodium content lest they cause you to drink more water than usual.

- Keep a stash of emergency cash ($200 or more) in small bills in an accessible place. ATM machines and bankcards may not work immediately after a disaster.

- Keep your gasoline tank in your car at least half-full at all times.

- Do not watch movies that portray disasters common to your area. Your eyes and ears are the gateways to your soul—that is, your mind, will, and emotions. Guard them from the spirit of fear.

- Visit the American Red Cross website (www .redcross.org) for additional emergency preparedness tips and guidelines for particular disasters.

Preparing to the best of your ability will help ease feelings of helplessness. Although disasters are inevitable, exercise your faith and pray a hedge of protection around your property. There are many stories of people who have done so with miraculous results. Even when God sent a record-breaking hailstorm against Egypt during the time they held the Israelites captive, He protected His children and their property:

*And the hail struck throughout the whole land of
Egypt, all that was in the field, both man and beast; and
the hail struck every herb of the field and broke every tree
of the field. Only in the land of Goshen, where the children of Israel were, there was no hail* (Exodus 9:25-26).

It's time to confess and believe Psalm 121:7 (NLT):
"The LORD keeps you from all harm and watches over
your life."

Day 11

Fear of Terrorism

Do not be afraid of sudden terror,
Nor of trouble from the wicked when it comes.
PROVERBS 3:25

I'm sure you have a vivid memory of exactly where you were when you received news of the terrorist attacks on September 11, 2001. I cried for days even though I knew none of the victims. Life as we knew it changed in a single day.

However, we are still here. Our freedom is intact—although we must now submit to more inconveniences to maintain it. The terrorists did not win. Virginia Foxx, American politician, said it best: "A terrorist network that believes a nation so tested will fold under pressure of a few horrific acts may capture its attention, but will not achieve its submission."[14]

Fear Analysis

The fear of terrorism is rooted in the core fear of *pain and death* and *helplessness or losing control*. Terrorists, as the word implies, use violence or the threat of it to intimidate and instill panic and fear in a country's citizens to achieve their political goals. To the extent that the citizenry stop flying or gathering in places of potential terrorist attacks, we help terrorists achieve their goals.

Since 9/11, the United States and the global community are more attentive to the possibility of terrorist threats and have made great progress to prevent them. The U.S. government, through the National Counterterrorism Center (NCTC), is doing everything possible to combat national and international terrorism. The center is a collaboration of experts from over sixteen domestic and foreign agencies including the Central Intelligence Agency (CIA), the Federal Bureau of Investigation (FBI), Departments of State, Defense, and Homeland Security, and others. The 24/7 operation, established in 2004, analyzes and acts upon all intelligence regarding terrorist groups and potential terrorist attacks. They have foiled numerous terrorist plots since the center's inception.[15]

Action Plan

Despite NCTC's efforts and effectiveness, anxiety surrounding potential terrorism remains high, especially in large cities. What do we need to do to shake off our fears?

- Make specific plans to maximize the present. Come out of fear prison. Take to the airways of the world. "It's time to get back to life," said Lisa Beamer before boarding the same flight on which her husband had died on September 11. She was right. Several months ago, Darnell and I flew to New York City for a few days to celebrate his birthday. Frankly, I had avoided New York like the plague since 9/11. No way was I going to put myself in harm's way. Boy, was I in for a pleasant awakening. The sightseeing at the Empire State Building and the Statue of Liberty, the discount shopping, the walk in Central Park, and even the bustling crowds at Times Square, all combined to make it one of our most memorable trips ever. We felt so alive just being there. We vowed to return soon. I regret that I had allowed fear of terrorism to keep me away so long from one of the most fabulous cities in the world.

- Interact often with world travelers and other adventurous folks. Ask them to share their experiences as well as how they overcome any trepidation about travel. Avoid super cautious, fearful folks who have decided that hibernating is the only way to survive. Fear is contagious.

- Do not watch news reports of terrorist activity—especially as you plan a trip. You are likely to feel powerless and panicky each time you subject yourself to images of destruction and mayhem.

- Consider the odds. Between October 1999 and September 2009, according to data from the Bureau of Transportation Statistics, there were over ninety-nine million flights in the United States. There were six terrorist attacks, and only four of those were successful and resulted in 647 deaths. The odds of being a terrorism victim on a flight have been 1 in 10,408,947 over the past decade. By contrast, the odds of being struck by lightning in a given year are about 1 in 500,000.[16]

- Remember that God, not the NCTC, is our ultimate protector. He is our Strong Tower that we can run to when we feel threatened. Therefore, we must believe and steadfastly declare His Word: "The LORD shall preserve your going out and your coming in from this time forth, and even forevermore" (Psalm 121:8).

Day 12

Fear of Crime and Violence

You shall not be afraid of the terror by night,
Nor of the arrow that flies by day.
PSALM 91:5

Anne made a quick trip to the local mall one eve-
ning to pick up a gift for a friend. Cautious by nature,
she caught a glimpse of a man behind her as she headed
out the door of the mall for the parking lot. No one else
was around. She went with her instinct and immediately doubled back into the mall as if she had forgotten
something. Once inside, she waited near the door until
a group of shoppers came along headed for the parking
lot. She quickly joined them and made it safely to her car.

A few days later, she received a call from the local
police department. The mall security cameras had
revealed that a man had indeed been following her. The
police had apprehended him in a related incident involving another woman. They wanted to know if she could
identify him. Her healthy fear of crime allowed her to
respond wisely to impending danger.

Are you constantly looking over your shoulder? Do

you go out less frequently to avoid the risk of being robbed or attacked? Does the latest newscast make you even more anxious? Have you ever been a victim of crime or violence?

Fear Analysis

Fear of crime and violence stem from the core fear of *pain and death*. During times of high unemployment and economic uncertainty, criminal activity increases. It is logical and wise to be sensitive to potential danger and to take steps to ensure your safety. Notwithstanding, crime and violence are still *exceptions* to normal behavior; that's why they lead the daily newscasts. After all, would a headline titled "No Crimes Today!" pique your interest? Of course not! However, the constant barrage of such stories gives the impression that these events are never ending. Thus, millions live in dread of becoming a victim. The constant emotional arousal over what may never occur can have a negative impact on a person's physical and psychological health.

Action Plan

Here are some strategies for controlling your fear of becoming a victim and some practical, preventative moves to thwart potential perpetrators.

- Keep the news in perspective. Crime is not the daily experience of the masses; it is an exception. That's why it makes the news.

- Stay alert. Without becoming paranoid, be

conscious of your surroundings. Don't be distracted with cell phones, an abundance of packages, or other items. Have car keys ready when you approach your car. Open only the driver's door when you are alone; mindlessly opening all the doors automatically exposes you to risk. When approaching your car, quickly scan the area around and underneath it. Also, check the backseat before hopping in.

- Lock your car as soon as you are inside. Don't linger. You can snack, make phone calls, or admire your purchases later.

- Choose well-traveled paths when walking. Avoid shortcuts through alleys, stairwells, fields, or parking lots.

- Walk boldly and confidently. Look potential assailants in the eyes. Project an image that says, "Mess with me, and you'll be sorry!" Most are not looking for a challenge.

- Don't walk alone in unsafe places or at unsafe times. Sometimes, when out walking with my husband, I marvel at the women I see alone in almost deserted parks at predawn hours.

- Trust your instincts. Like Anne, if you feel something is amiss, change your direction.

- Keep the importance of your stuff in perspective. If a robber wants it, let him have it without a fight. Everything can be replaced.

- If someone tries to abduct you, don't go like a sheep to the slaughter; become a wildcat and do everything possible to resist, draw attention, and avoid getting into his vehicle.

- Program 911 or other emergency number into your cell phone for quick access.

- Keep your car well-maintained and with at least a third of a tank of gasoline. A stalled car is a beacon for criminals.

- If you think you're being followed, drive to a police station or a well-lit gas station.

- Vary your routine. Occasionally take a different route to and from work. Adjust your departure and arrival times as well.

- Don't become lax in setting the alarm on your home security system. When our home was burglarized, our front gate was wide open and the security system was inoperable.

- Stand strong in faith and pray a hedge of protection around yourself daily. Memorize the following passage and recite it often:

The LORD says, "I will rescue those who love me.
I will protect those who trust in my name.
When they call on me, I will answer;
I will be with them in trouble.
I will rescue and honor them.
I will reward them with a long life
and give them my salvation."

(PSALM 91:14-16 NLT)

Part 2
Relational Fears

Day 13

Fear of Loneliness

*"The worst loneliness is not to be
comfortable with yourself."*
MARK TWAIN

Wolfgang Dircks, a divorced, disabled loner, was
found dead in his apartment in Bonn, Germany in
December 1998—five years after he passed away. Dircks
apparently died in 1993 at age forty-three while watch-
ing television. Neighbors in the apartment complex
where he resided hardly noticed his absence. The land-
lord came knocking only after the bank account from
which his rent and bills were paid ran dry. A TV listings
magazine was still sitting on the lap of Dircks's skeleton
and was open to the page for December 5, 1993—the
presumed date of his death. The television set had long
since stopped in the on position, but the lights on his
1993 Christmas tree were still twinkling away.[1]

The fact that Dircks lived *alone* does not necessarily mean that he was *lonely*. It's important to understand
the difference. *Aloneness* is a *physical* state of voluntary or
circumstantial solitude or isolation due to divorce, death,

confinement, relocation, or some other cause; *loneliness* is an *emotional* state in which a person feels disconnected, isolated, alienated, or cut off from meaningful interaction with others.

Habitual aloneness is not God's will for His children. Adam had an ideal environment in the Garden of Eden. Further, he was a man of keen intellect as demonstrated by his ability to name every single animal. Yet God declared, "It is not good that man should be alone; I will make him a helper comparable to him" (Genesis 2:18). Yes, some animals can help alleviate loneliness, but God created man to be in relationship with those "comparable" to him. Loneliness is an emotionally painful state that causes great anxiety. Many go to great lengths to avoid it.

A 1990 Gallup study indicated that about 36 percent of Americans are lonely. Sociologists generally agree that the baby boomer generation (born 1946–1964) is headed for a crisis of loneliness as more of them live alone, marry less, divorce more, move or relocate frequently, or simply prefer the convenience of not having to consider the needs of another.

Fear Analysis

The fear of loneliness or being alone is a core fear known by a number of names including autophobia, isolaphobia, and monophobia. It is the root of many unwise decisions and counterproductive behavior. It can significantly affect a person's quality of life physically, emotionally, relationally, and financially. Studies show that this fear makes people insecure, anxious, clingy, and depressed. It causes them to tolerate dysfunctional or abusive relationships.

Many people are lonely though not alone, such as when there is an emotionally unavailable spouse or fiancé. Often a person who fears loneliness will lavish gifts (affordable or unaffordable) on undeserving people. Such relationships are unfulfilling, but many conclude that they are less painful than the emptiness of loneliness.

All of us may experience occasional loneliness; however, chronic loneliness can be lethal. It has been associated with an increased risk of death from cancer as well as stroke and cardiovascular disease.

Action Plan

You do not have to accept loneliness as your unavoidable destiny. Try these proactive strategies for ensuring a meaningful and rewarding social network.

- Expand your interests. Learning to enjoy and engage in more activities will give you a broader base of social interactions. Book clubs, bowling leagues, Bible study groups, and exercise classes are great places to start.

- Be generous to others—not just with your finances. This is not a call to excessive spending designed to buy friends, but a challenge to serve others with your time, talents, and treasure when needed. "A man who has friends must himself be friendly, but there is a friend who sticks closer than a brother" (Proverbs 18:24).

- Show a genuine interest in the problems of others. Guard against making your issues and concerns the focus of every conversation. "Do nothing out of selfish ambition or vain conceit. Rather, in humility value others above yourselves, not looking to your own interests but each of you to the interests of the others" (Philippians 2:4 NIV).

- Practice being accepting of others versus being judgmental. People love to interact with folks who accept them "as is."

- Put an end to your voluntary social isolation. Begin nurturing your relationships by connecting with at least three people each week via phone or in person. Don't get sucked into the "Facebook/email/text message only" communication vacuum. Commit to visiting with close friends, family, or even a neighbor or two at established intervals (biweekly, quarterly, and so on). I have three long-time friends from my employment at a CPA firm over thirty years ago. We meet at least three to four times a year for lunch and laughter— and sharing our personal concerns. I also have extended conversations at least twice monthly with three other close friends who live out of state. This requires t-i-m-e, but it is worth it. *Caution:* Don't try to nurture a relationship that doesn't nurture you. Meaningful relationships must be mutually satisfying.

- Work at being comfortable with solitude and aloneness. Take time to enjoy your favorite dish, movie, or other activity alone. See it as a personal treat; others will be attracted to your independence and confidence. The Scriptures record numerous instances of Jesus resorting to solitude for meditation, renewal, and reflection (see Matthew 14:23; Mark 1:35; Luke 4:42; 5:16). Solitude is detrimental only when taken to excess.

- Reject the idea that you cannot survive without a certain person being in your life. God is the only one you *must* have, and He has promised never to leave you. Many spouses have fallen into protracted periods of depression after the death of their mates because they had not cultivated an outside life. It's never too late to get started.

- Resist the temptation to banish people from your life who have offended you. Extend to them the forgiveness God continues to extend to you. They may be the very ones who add zest to your life later.

Day 14

Fear of Commitment

*"There's only one way to succeed in anything,
and that is to give it everything."*
VINCE LOMBARDI,
LEGENDARY FOOTBALL COACH

The definition of *commit* ("to bind, obligate, pledge")
conjures up images of bondage, restrictions, and loss of
freedom. It's a word that frightens many.

Take Dan X for instance. He has lived with his girl-
friend, Darlene Y, for over thirty-six years. They have
three beautiful daughters and several grandchildren. I
asked Dan over ten years ago why he had never married
Darlene. "Her mother is very controlling and wields a lot
of power over her," he said. "No way am I going to battle for first place in her life."

A few years ago, Darlene's mother passed away. Dan
still made no move to formalize their relationship. The
truth is, Dan is afraid of commitment, not only to a
long-term romantic relationship but to anything that
requires an extended obligation—even a home mortgage. Thus they continue to live in a cramped apartment,

and Darlene has given up hope of ever wearing his last name or owning a home.

Fear Analysis

Commitment fear often centers on what freedoms, privileges, or resources a person believes he might lose and what unknowns he might encounter. For brevity, we will limit this discussion to romantic relationships.

The noncommitting partner's fear is rooted in the core fears of *losing control* (Why give up my independence?), *lack* (What if she drives my finances into the ground?), *inadequacy* (Can I meet her expectations?), *loneliness* (Suppose he deserts me?), and fear of *pain* (I don't want to repeat an emotional hurt). Dan and Darlene are like millions of commitment-phobic, cohabitating couples. Because one or both partners fear the unknown, they decide to live together first in a "trial marriage."

However, living together without marriage can be compared to renting a room versus buying a home. If a repair is needed to the rented room, the renters are likely to abandon the room in favor of another. If a repair is required for their home, the owners make the necessary commitment to protect their investment.

Psychology Today reported the findings of Yale University sociologist Neil Bennett that cohabiting women who subsequently married were 80 percent more likely to separate or divorce than were women who had not lived with their spouses before marriage.[2] In today's society, many women (especially the economically empowered ones) are reluctant to make a commitment to a man.

Notwithstanding, it is usually the man who wants to keep the relationship fluid and flexible so that he can exercise his stay-or-leave option at will. The partner desiring the commitment finds such relationships frustrating and unfulfilling.

Action Plan

A relationship without commitment is like a stamp without glue. If you are ready to banish your qualms about committing, try these strategies:

- Commit to being honest with yourself first and then to others about your feelings and motivations. Meditate on Psalm 51:6: "Behold, You desire truth in the inward parts, and in the hidden part You will make me to know wisdom."

- Determine what specific circumstance, event, or situation triggered your fear of commitment (e.g., early childhood observation of bad examples (primarily parents), negative experience in a previous romantic relationship, or observation of a friend's negative experience). Have you observed a similar pattern of behavior on your part or that of a potential mate?

- Acknowledge the role you played, even as an enabler of bad behavior, in the failure of a previous relationship. Are you different now? Are you willing to change?

- Consider whether you have genuine feelings for your partner or whether you may be biding time until someone better comes along or becomes free from another relationship.

- Discuss your specific fears with your partner: "I'm afraid you'll try to change me"; "I'll feel emasculated if you don't submit to me"; "If the marriage fails, you may take my money and leave me impoverished"; "You may restrict too much of my time with the boys"; "You may become obese"; "You may require too much of my attention." Solicit his or her feedback to your concerns.

- Try a thirty-day (or more) period of "no contact" with your romantic interest and see how life would be without him or her. Some non-committed relationships are just for convenience, so evaluate your feelings apart from the inconvenience you'll suffer. Convenience is an unstable foundation for a marriage.

- Reevaluate your expectations. Don't expect your partner to fulfill every aspect of your life. For example, you may have to satisfy your need for high adventure with brave friends and be content that your partner is loyal, loving, and laughs a lot. Of course, recreational companionship is important to most men, so it's wise to agree on mutually satisfying activities (e.g., hiking or boating versus rock climbing or skydiving).

- If you have discussed and tolerated your partner's deal-breaking behavior with no repentance in sight, break the deal and cut your losses now. Reread chapter 13, "Fear of Loneliness."

- If there are no deal-breaking behaviors or issues in your relationship, but you simply fear the unknown, use your faith to bridge the gap between your qualms and the peace you desire. Don't manufacture reasons not to commit; stop nitpicking every imperfection. Establish with your partner what the deal-breaking issues are (abuse, infidelity), then move forward with your commitment. Give the Great Counselor a chance to show Himself strong in your life. Don't tolerate a relationship that is dishonoring to God. The only sexually intimate relationship that is pleasing to God is one based on a formal commitment before Him to stick together for better or for worse. I have enjoyed a fulfilling, committed relationship with my husband for over thirty-two years. Yes, each of us pondered many "what ifs" before we said "I do." In the final analysis, we knew the success of our relationship would hinge on our commitment to put God first and do marriage His way.

Day 15

Fear of Intimacy

*"To say 'I love you' one must know
first how to say the 'I'."*
AYN RAND, RUSSIAN-AMERICAN
NOVELIST, PHILOSOPHER

Adam and Eve experienced it—until they sinned. Naked and unashamed, they were totally vulnerable with each other. After the fall, they covered their nakedness with fig leaves (Genesis 2:25; 3:7). Samson made the tragic assumption that he had it with Delilah. When he told her that his hair was the secret to his strength, she betrayed him and had it shaved off in exchange for a bribe from his enemies (Judges 16). Jesus shared it with His disciples, calling them "friends" instead of servants (John 15:15).

Intimacy. It is the close, familiar, and usually affectionate or loving personal connection with another person or group. Emotional intimacy is the bedrock of any meaningful and rewarding relationship. Without it, relationships become shallow and unfulfilling.

Fear Analysis

Millions of people desire intimacy, but the prospect of revealing to others our fears, needs, insecurities, secrets, hopes, dreams, weird opinions, or our undesirable parts can be scary. The fear of intimacy is rooted in the fear of *loneliness* ("If you really knew me, you'd leave me"), the fear of *inadequacy* ("I may be exposed as the imposter I feel I am"), and the fear of *losing control* ("Now that she knows how I feel, she may use it to control me").

Fear of intimacy differs from fear of commitment. It can be compared to how we treat visitors versus intimate friends. Most visitors to my home remain downstairs in the living or family room; I've simply committed to letting them in the house. When my close friends visit me, I invite them upstairs to see my latest window treatment project, photos, plants, or whatever. This invitation is reserved for special people, and they enjoy the privilege. That's how your spouse, close friends, and others feel when you allow them "upstairs" in your emotions.

Emotional intimacy is one of the greatest gifts you can give someone. The experience of intimacy fills their souls and yours—and eliminates their loneliness. Why let fear cause you to deny others such a rewarding opportunity? And yes, men, the Bible suggests emotional intimacy between men. The elders of the church in Ephesus, realizing they would never see Paul again, "wept freely, and fell on Paul's neck and kissed him" (Acts 20:37). This scene is in sharp contrast to how men are socialized in the American culture to squash such emotions.

Nevertheless, so-called "tough guys" need warmth and affection like everyone else. Don't be in denial about this. It will add years to your life and life to your years.

Action Plan

Famed athlete Bill Russell says, "Most people have a harder time letting themselves love than finding someone to love them." If you are ready to banish your qualms about intimacy, try these strategies:

- Understand the source for your fear. What really happened to make you avoid a desire to be known?

- Accept yourself completely—every feature, every imperfection—as God's masterpiece; now you can stop worrying about someone rejecting you because you're not perfect.

- Test the waters. Start gradually with a few close, accepting friends and begin to share how you feel about certain social or political issues. No need to be dogmatic about them. Later, try expanding the conversation to your childhood trials and triumphs.

- Confess your struggle with your weight, self-image, or other issues. Stop pretending you wear a smaller size. Ask for support. Find the joy in being authentic.

- Practice saying "I love you" to the significant

people in your life even if it feels foreign to do so. So what if you never had it said to you? Stop fearing. "I love you" does not translate "I want to be your slave," nor does it say, "I'll tolerate anything to remain in relationship with you."

- Don't allow your fear of intimacy to produce uncertainty and isolation in your marriage. Many women assume that a man's detached demeanor is an indication of infidelity. God has ordained marriage to be a source of support, stability, and closeness. Practice expressing and demonstrating your care and concern. I consider it an act of intimacy when my husband is concerned enough to take my car to the mechanic, especially since it would be more convenient for me to do so.

- Know that nagging, being critical, and similar behaviors are enemies to intimacy.

Day 16

Fear of Rejection

*"There's nothing like rejection to make
you do an inventory of yourself."*
JAMES LEE BURKE, AMERICAN AUTHOR

No one is above being rejected. Even God and Jesus experienced it. The Israelites, God's chosen people, rejected His rule over them in favor of an earthly king so they could be like other nations. Their attitude was, "Enough of the judges!" God responded by granting them their request for a king. He comforted Samuel, the reigning judge, who felt personally rejected. "And the LORD said to Samuel, 'Heed the voice of the people in all that they say to you; for they have not rejected you, but they have rejected Me, that I should not reign over them'"(1 Samuel 8:7). He further instructed Samuel to advise them of the dire consequences of being ruled by an earthly king (1 Samuel 8:9-18).

The people of Nazareth rejected Jesus and His ministry simply because He had grown up there and they were familiar with Him and His family (Mark 6:1-6). The old adage "familiarity breeds contempt" was never more evident. Jesus didn't sit around and lick His emotional wounds; He simply moved on to where people gladly received Him.

Fear Analysis

Fear of rejection is a common fear rooted in the core fears of *loneliness* and the fear of *inadequacy*. Rejection can leave you feeling isolated; it also tends to validate your belief that you are inadequate. It is natural to fear rejection if you place a high value on certain people and how they feel about you.

In my younger days, I often succumbed to this fear, saying yes to requests when I really wanted to say no; going along to get along. The prospect of being isolated seemed like a death sentence. The irony in operating out of fear of rejection is that it ultimately results in the very rejection you are trying to avoid. When people realize you hold yourself in low regard, they deal with you accordingly. *You teach people how to value you by how you value yourself.* If you never express a preference, a boundary, or any other limitation on how others interact with you, they will likely assume you have none and behave toward you in that manner. Notice that even though God and Jesus were rejected, neither responded in a way that encouraged continued rejection.

Action Plan

The keys to conquering fear of rejection lie within you. Here's how to break free:

• The most critical step to overcoming this fear is to embrace every part of your being with an *individualistic* mindset. You must believe that you are uniquely designed (physically, intellectually, temperamentally) and put on this earth for a specific purpose. You must not reject any aspect of God's design or His plan for you. You must be fully persuaded and emphatically declare, as did the psalmist,

> *For You formed my inward parts;*
> *You covered me in my mother's womb.*
> *I will praise You, for I am fearfully and*
>   *wonderfully made;*
> *Marvelous are Your works,*
> *And that my soul knows very well.*
> *My frame was not hidden from You,*
> *When I was made in secret,*
> *And skillfully wrought in the lowest parts*
>   *of the earth.*
> *Your eyes saw my substance, being*
>   *yet unformed.*
> *And in Your book they all were written,*
> *The days fashioned for me,*
> *When as yet there were none of them.*

(PSALM 139:13-16)

• Now that you have the big picture, determine when and where the idea originated that you are inferior or "less than" whatever person or group you fear will reject you. Whether it started with critical parents, unwise teachers, cruel classmates, or a verbally abusive spouse, remember that Satan is the father of *all* lies (John 8:44). He used someone to lie to you about your worth or potential. Repeat, "It was a lie! It was a lie! It was a lie!" Decide to reject the lie now! (One of my mentors used to say, "Reject rejection!").

- Make a list of every God-given gift, asset, advantage, or other benefit you possess that is or could be a blessing to others. Don't use worldly values in developing this list. Focus on character issues such as integrity, loyalty, generosity, and patience. Think of ways you can use each one to glorify God and improve someone's life.

- Be your authentic self when you are with others. Focus on what you have to give rather than how they perceive you. Don't put on airs, brag, or name-drop in an attempt to level the playing field. You are already equal— even if you don't have a similar education, experience, financial status, social standing, or background. Since when did such things make anybody inherently superior to another—especially in the eyes of your heavenly Father?

- Spend time with people who like and affirm

you; avoid the critical folks who only rein-
force your sense of inadequacy.

- Don't keep quiet for peace sake. Confront
behavior that negatively affects you. Jesus
commanded it (Matthew 18:15; Luke 17:3).
Visit www.confrontingissues.com for tips and
resources on how to do this effectively.

- If you do encounter rejection, do as Jesus did.
Move on—and thank God that He slammed
the door on the relationship. Adopt the mindset of the Proverbs 31 woman and "perceive
that [your] merchandise is good" (v. 18).

- Respect other people's decision not to pursue
a relationship with you. Think about the last
time you went shopping. Did you purchase
every single item you examined? Of course
not. Did you reject them because they were
inferior? Surely not. You simply decided they
were not for you. Of course, if you see a pattern of rejection, and you are baffled about
the cause, you may want to consider finding
out why. For example, you may call up a former friend or boyfriend and say, "Listen, I'd
like to get some feedback from you for my
personal development. My objective here is
not to resume our relationship. I would just
like to ask what it was that made you decide
to terminate our relationship? I'd really

appreciate your honest feedback." Be sure to project an upbeat attitude. Listen objectively and don't be defensive; you are gathering information. Be willing to change if there is merit to their input.

Day 17

Fear of Losing a Loved One

"For the thing I greatly feared has come upon me,
And what I dreaded has happened to me."
Job 3:25

If you were a godly parent with ten children who loved to party, it would only be natural to be concerned about their relationship with the Almighty. Meet Job. He was a righteous rich man. He owned seven thousand sheep, three thousand camels, five hundred yoke of oxen, five hundred donkeys, and had a large number of servants.

Despite his holdings, his primary concern was that his children might one day offend God with their partying and suffer His wrath. Job's anxiety led him to offer sacrifices to God on his children's behalf to "purify" them after each time of feasting. "Early in the morning he would sacrifice a burnt offering for each of them, thinking, 'Perhaps my children have sinned and cursed God in their hearts.' This was Job's regular custom" (Job 1:5 NIV).

One day, all hell broke loose. Three different messengers brought successive news reports that raiders and fire from heaven had wiped out all Job's livestock as well as the attending servants. The fourth messenger brought the most dreaded news. The oldest son's house, where his children had been feasting, had collapsed during a fierce windstorm. None of them had escaped. Seven sons... three daughters...all gone in one day. Job would later lament, "For the thing I greatly feared has come upon me, and what I dreaded has happened to me" (Job 3:25).

Fear Analysis

The fear of losing a loved one is rooted in the core fears of *(emotional) pain and death, loneliness, losing control*, and even *fear of financial devastation* as the loved one may have been the only source of financial support. By no means am I suggesting a selfish motive may be the main cause of your anxiety, but the possibility of an economic loss and the uncertainty of future income can be dreaded issues.

As painful an exercise as this may be, I ask you to consider the one person whose death you dread the most. Does the thought of losing him or her regularly cause you great anxiety? Do you realize that you are sabotaging today's joy by anticipating future emotional pain?

Action Plan

Here are some suggestions for getting the fear of losing a loved one under control so you can live in peace, free from needless worry.

• Ask God for the grace to accept that death is

an inevitable part of life. You and your loved ones will eventually die, and no one except God knows who is going to do so first. Therefore, worrying about something outside your control only robs you of today's quality of life.

- Determine what aspect of the loss you least want to face: loss of the person's companionship, unconditional love, listening ear, or other. Consider whether your anxiety about losing the person is a sign that you need to broaden your interests or deepen your relationship with others so that you are not all alone when he or she is gone.

- Maximize the moment. Think about what you would do if you knew time was very short for your loved one. What would you stop doing? Would you plan that trip you've always dreamed about taking? Would you stop being so critical of him? Would you be more inclined to express your feelings toward her? Would you find more time to visit him?

- Daily commit to maintaining an amicable relationship with your loved ones so that you have no need for regret when they pass on. My longtime boyfriend from high school died in a car accident during my junior year in college. For years after, I lived with the remorse that my last conversation with him had ended with my hanging up on him after a silly argument. I now make every effort to reconcile all conflicts in a godly and timely manner with my husband and others.

- Make every effort to assure that your loved one is in right standing with God through the blood of Jesus. Then you can rest assured that she is at peace and that you will spend eternity together.

- If your loved one's death is imminent, spend as much time with him as possible during his final days. I'll always cherish the memory of the 37 days I spent with my father before he transitioned to heaven.

- Remember that your loved one is God's loved one also. Ask for grace to trust His decision regarding that person's lifespan. When the time comes to grieve your loss, know that your heavenly Father will be right there supplying the grace you need and giving you inexplicable peace. "Cast your burden on the LORD, and He shall sustain you" (Psalm 55:22).

- Renounce the spirit of fear. Jesus died so you would not have to suffer that fear.

Because God's children are human beings—made of flesh and blood—the Son also became flesh and blood.

For only as a human being could he die, and only by dying could he break the power of the devil, who had the power of death. Only in this way could he set free all who have lived their lives as slaves to the fear of dying (Hebrews 2:14-15 NLT).

Day 18

Fear of Social Situations

Be anxious for nothing, but in everything by
prayer and supplication, with thanksgiving,
let your requests be made known to God;
and the peace of God, which surpasses all
understanding, will guard your hearts
and minds through Christ Jesus.

PHILIPPIANS 4:6-7

We are hardwired to be social creatures, to fellow-ship with others. Even though our God-given temperament influences how we interact with people, our life's experiences play a huge role in the development of our social skills.

Take Laverne, for example. She suffered disfiguring acne from her teenage to early adult years. Her critical mother told her she looked hideous. She assumed that everyone else judged her looks similarly. She rarely made eye contact with others for fear of scorn. She finally discovered a treatment that corrected her acne-scarred skin, but the emotional scars remained. She became reclusive except for going to work. The thought of attending her company's social gatherings made her panicky. When coworkers tried to engage her in conversation, she gave curt answers to shorten the interaction time, which they perceived as rude. Laverne's fear of socializing had put her on the fast track to isolation. When the pain of loneliness became unbearable, she sought help. She has now tamed the fear that once controlled her.

Fear Analysis

Fear of socializing is rooted in the core fears of *inadequacy* and *loneliness*. It is characterized by the avoidance of situations where one feels she will be scrutinized or judged negatively by others. The trigger for this fear can often be traced to adolescence or simply a lack of exposure to social opportunities. Millions suffer from fear of socializing, which goes beyond mere shyness.

While my colleagues may consider me socially adept, I often experience anxiety when I know that I'll be socializing with "intellectual giants" who can philosophize about world issues. I try to keep abreast of the news and maintain a general grasp of political issues by listening to both conservative and liberal talk shows. I am versed in the rules of social etiquette and networking (even wrote a popular book on it!). I have a good command of English and can articulate my thoughts.

However, when I'm around political pundits or other experts, I fear I'm going to say something that makes me look as though I don't have a clue about the real issue. I know that the key to surviving these situations is to ask questions and let other folks look smart, but I often fret that even asking a question will cause them to wonder why I don't know the answer already. Surely, they'll reject me as a conversational equal.

When I find myself going down such a self-focused path in my thinking, I immediately halt the negative imaginings and start the self-talk: *Hey, Deborah, no one here is better than you. Your input is as valuable as anyone else's. You can't know everything. You are not intellectually or socially inferior to anyone. Now get back in the game and have a great time!*

Action Plan

There are no shortcuts to overcoming fear of socializing. You're going to have to work to become comfortable being with people. Here are some sure-fire strategies:

- Stop confessing that you have social phobia. Why own something so destructive to your goals and relationships? Reject that spirit. "For God has not given us a spirit of fear, but of power and of love and of a sound mind" (2 Timothy 1:7).

- Pursue an activity you really enjoy so that you'll have something to talk about with passion. no mind reading.

- Show up. The fact that you have labeled yourself "shy" is no reason to shy away from opportunities to overcome it. Avoidance reinforces the fear.

- Ignore your pounding heart, shaky voice,

- perspiration, upset stomach, or other symptoms of anxiety; they are not fatal.

- Smile. It's contagious and essential to looking approachable.

- Set a goal of initiating a conversation with at least two or three people at any social event. Increase the number as you become more confident.

- Introduce yourself; say your name slowly and confidently.

- Thwart self-consciousness by focusing on others. Ask nonpersonal, nonprying questions to get them to talk about their favorite subject—themselves. Really listen to them and respond to their answers rather than worrying about what you'll ask next.

- Remember that you may be able to *influence* what people think about you, but you cannot *control* it—so stop thinking about their evaluation or approval of you.

- Meditate on Philippians 4:6-7 and let the peace of God rule in your heart.

Once you become more socially secure, you open the door to a whole new world of opportunities—and more fun!

Part 3

Psychological Fears

Day 19

Fear of Inadequacy

"My grace is sufficient for you, for My strength is made perfect in weakness."
2 Corinthians 12:9

I couldn't believe my eyes when I saw the conference agenda. The meeting planners had scheduled me to be the last speaker! Isn't it traditional to save the best for last? My heart started to race.

Speaker A was a highly regarded, internationally known powerhouse with a fiery delivery and an engaging, heart-rending personal story of abandonment and drug addiction. Speaker B was also well-known and had an awe-inspiring rags-to-riches testimony. As Speaker C, I felt I had nothing to say that would really wow the audience. After all, my parents had never abandoned me, I never tried drugs, I was raised in church, finished college, married a wonderful man, and pursued a great career in corporate America. Of course, I'd had some physical and emotional pain along the way, but nothing paralleling the stories of the other speakers. I could just imagine one giant audience yawn if I were to give *that* testimony.

The sight of thousands of expectant faces waiting for me to say something profound made my heart race even more. I felt an overwhelming sense of inadequacy—until I remembered to practice what I preach. My own words echoed in my mind, *I am indeed inadequate. We are all inadequate in our own strength!* Jesus said so. "I am the vine, you are the branches. He who abides in Me, and I in him, bears much fruit; for without Me you can do nothing" (John 15:5). When I locked my thoughts on this truth, I felt supreme confidence begin to infuse my heart. I delivered a life-changing message that day—according to subsequent emails from many attendees.

Fear Analysis

Fear of inadequacy is one of the five core fears (discussed in the Prologue) that dictate the quality of our lives. As a core fear, it is also the bedrock of a number of other fears discussed in this book. This debilitating state of mind in which we think we are not good enough usually originates in childhood as our parents, teachers, others we deem important, and even ourselves unwisely compare our performance or appearance to that of others. Inadequacy is triggered in us as adults by the same tendency to compare or to fail to meet certain expectations (even unrealistic ones promoted by the media).

From Moses, who felt inadequate to be the spokesperson and deliverer for the Israelites, to the late pop star Michael Jackson, who pursued physical and professional perfection, fear of inadequacy has been the scourge of mankind. No statistics can measure the number of abandoned dreams due to this paralyzing emotion. To rid ourselves of it, we must learn how to embrace two overriding truths: (1) we are inadequate *apart* from God, and (2) we are more than conquerors *with* Him.

Action Plan

Try these strategies to move from fear of inadequacy to assurance of sufficiency:

- Understand that making us feel inadequate is big business. Be on guard for the "you or your current possession is inadequate" message in commercials or advertisements. Know when you are being set up to "buy adequacy."

- Stop the self-rejection. You are not too old, too young, too ugly, too pretty, too dark, too fair, too dumb, too educated—too anything. You are custom designed for a unique destiny. Begin to declare, "I will praise You, for I am fearfully and wonderfully made" (Psalm 139:14).

- View the excellence or superior performance of another as a source of motivation rather than intimidation. Meanwhile, don't lose sight of your unique giftedness (yes, you are gifted in *some* area).

- Readily confess your inadequacy to God. Joni Eareckson Tada says, "Deny your weakness, and you will never realize God's strength in you."

- Show up for the task. God is always on the lookout for a vessel through whom He can show His strength. "For the eyes of the LORD run to and fro throughout the whole earth, to show Himself strong on behalf of those whose heart is loyal to Him" (2 Chronicles 16:9).

- Anticipate the spiritual intimacy that results from depending on Him. One of my most significant periods of spiritual growth came when I accepted a job that was way over my head. Experiencing God's revelation and guidance during that period resulted in a great shift in my thinking. I realized I could never acquire all the knowledge I'll need to succeed. Therefore, I must maintain an intimate connection with my all-knowing Father. Imagine being connected to an omniscient being who loves you and wants the best for you.

- Memorize and meditate often on 2 Corinthians 3:5: "Not that we are sufficient of ourselves to think of anything as being from ourselves, but our sufficiency is from God." This passage confirms that adequacy does not emanate *from* you but rather flows *through* you.

Day 20

Fear of Public Speaking

*"You can speak well if your tongue can
deliver the message of your heart."*
JOHN FORD, AMERICAN FILM DIRECTOR

Moses couldn't fathom being the chosen spokes-person to persuade Pharaoh to release the Israelites from bondage. Surely, God knew about his embarrassing speech impediment. Let's listen in on their dialogue:

> But Moses pleaded with the LORD, "O Lord, I'm not very good with words. I never have been, and I'm not now, even though you have spoken to me. I get tongue-tied, and my words get tangled."
>
> Then the LORD asked Moses, "Who makes a person's mouth? Who decides whether people speak or do not speak, hear or do not hear, see or do not see? Is it not I, the LORD? Now go! I will be with you as you speak, and I will instruct you in what to say."
>
> But Moses again pleaded, "Lord, please! Send anyone else" (EXODUS 4:10-13 NLT).

Not even God could convince Moses that he was

capable of fulfilling the speaking aspect of his historic assignment. God became angry with Moses, and finally agreed that Moses would do the leading and his brother Aaron would be his spokesperson (Exodus 4:14-16).

Fear Analysis

Moses was not alone. According to Toastmasters International, glossophobia, the fear of public speaking, is number one of all human fears. It is rooted in the core fears of *inadequacy* and *loneliness* (isolation). Most people get anxious when required to speak to a group because they are afraid of being humiliated, of looking foolish, or even panicking and drawing a blank. Perhaps they remember an embarrassing childhood experience in which the whole class laughed at them as they stood up front, or the panic they felt when they forgot their line in the school play. Such events can scar your confidence for a lifetime if you don't "jump back on the bicycle" and ride it again.

Because I tend to speak rapidly, I used to fear when giving a speech that I would run out of material before my allotted time was up and have nothing else to say. On a few occasions this has happened, despite timing my speeches beforehand. However, the grace of God has covered me with "on the spot" information and insight each time as I have shifted into faith mode.

I admit it can be a little scary. Nevertheless, I know that goals and objectives are accomplished by communicating with people—sometimes large groups at a time. No leader or anyone desiring to achieve anything meaningful in life can afford to succumb to this fear by avoiding public speaking opportunities. Further, allowing fear, shyness, or self-consciousness to keep us from sharing the information God has entrusted to us is the epitome of pride and self-centeredness. Unfortunately, many people decide that man's opinion or evaluation is more important than God's purpose. "The fear of man brings a snare, but whoever trusts in the LORD shall be safe" (Proverbs 29:25).

Action Plan

When a group invites you to speak, they have already concluded that you can deliver the goods. You don't have to be a great orator with a huge vocabulary. You simply have to deliver a message. You do not have to emulate any other speaker; you just have to decide to be the best "you" possible. Try the strategies below and soon you will find public speaking to be an invigorating and satisfying experience.

- Stick to subjects for which you have a passion or related experience.

- Thoroughly research your topic. Get the facts; find illustrations, anecdotes, and simple statistics that bring life and practical application to your points. Internet search engines, such as Google, are a speaker's dream. Simply input your topic and a host of resources will appear. Remember, confidence is rooted in knowledge. The more you know about your topic, the more confident you will be.

- Don't over prepare. Limit your speech to three points. Actually, one principle or big idea thoroughly researched and supported with great stories or examples will be even more memorable.

- Settle on the purpose of the speech. Do you want to inform, inspire, persuade? Whatever your objective, know that the information must be presented in an interesting and entertaining fashion to hold the audience's attention.

- Check out the place where you'll be speaking. If possible, stand at the lectern and with the eyes of your faith, envision yourself delivering a powerful message and having a great time to boot. See everyone in attendance soaking up the value of your words.

- Wear an appropriate and attractive outfit that makes you feel confident. This is not the time to be distracted by self-consciousness.

- Forget about messing up. Chances are that you will know more about the topic of your speech than 90 percent of the audience. If you stumble, so what? It signals the audience that you are human—just as they are. People will connect better with your vulnerability than your strength. Besides, they are rooting for you. They want you to succeed.

- Rather than using postcards, print speaking notes (using at least 16-point type) on regular 8.5 by 11 paper. Punch holes and anchor the sheets in a one-inch, three-ring binder to eliminate the possibility of dropping them during your presentation. Many speakers have experienced the embarrassment of trying to collect and reorganize postcards that have fallen and scattered on the floor.

- Don't be a slave to the notes. After a few speeches in which you write out every word, start using only an outline with key facts and examples. Just practice being familiar with the information.

- Create a bond with the audience during the critical first three minutes of your speech (based on information you have already obtained about them). Humility will take you a long way here. Try making a candid confession (use discretion), telling a story, asking for a show of hands to a question, complimenting the audience, or using humor. A word of caution: Tell a joke only if it is really funny and you are good at delivering a punch line; test the suitability of the joke on your friends first.

- Focus on imparting value to the audience rather than trying to impress them or getting stressed over how they perceive you.

- Maintain good eye contact; focus on the friendly faces to maintain confidence.

- Don't belabor a point. If you notice people looking around, doodling, or talking to one another, conclude your point and move on to another—or to the conclusion. Vary the pitch of your voice often. Time your stories to break the monotony of facts.

- During your speech, deal with symptoms of nervousness as they occur. Dr. Paul Witt, communications professor at Texas Christian University suggests the following:[1]

  - Dry mouth? Take a little sip of water.

  - Knees knocking? Shift your weight and flex your knees.

  - Hands trembling? Put them together.

  - Voice quivering? Pause, take a deep breath or two, and smile. It is amazing what a smile will do.

  - Sweating? Forget it, nobody sees that anyway.

- Keep running toward your fear of public speaking. Accept every formal and informal opportunity to hone your skills. Consider joining your local Toastmasters International club (www.toastmasters.com), a world leader in helping people become more competent and comfortable in front of an audience. Practice. Practice. Practice.

- If you are asked to bring a biblically based message—a Word from God—do not rely on your intellect only. My now-deceased mentor always warned, "Prepare as if it all depends on you; but when you present, know that it all depends on God." Yes, preparation is essential, but you must learn to rely on the Holy Spirit for the words you'll speak. The apostle Paul proclaimed, "And my speech and my preaching was not with enticing words of man's wisdom, but in demonstration of the Spirit and of power: that your faith should not stand in the wisdom of men, but in the power of God" (1 Corinthians 2:4-5 KJV).

Day 21

Fear of Gaining Weight

You were bought at a price; therefore
glorify God in your body and in
your spirit, which are God's.

1 CORINTHIANS 6:20

On July 26, 1994, American gymnast Christy Henrich died from multiple organ-system failure. Christy, ranked the number two gymnast in the country, had represented the United States at the 1989 World Championships in Germany. That same year, an international judge told her she was fat (compared to the new trend of small, underweight, prepubescent gymnasts) and needed to lose weight. She took the criticism to heart. Her drive to lose a few pounds progressed to unhealthy eating habits and, eventually, full-blown anorexia nervosa.

The eating disorder took such a toll on her health that she was no longer strong enough to compete and was asked to leave the gym in 1991. When her weight dropped to around forty-seven pounds, her family intervened and compelled her to enter hospital treatment. In spite of numerous treatments and periods of recovery,

Christy died eight days after her twenty-second birthday. Her heart, liver, and lungs simply stopped working.[2]

Annie, a twenty-nine-year-old financial manager, comes from a background of obese relatives. She has battled her weight since junior high school. However, through constant dieting and exercise, she has managed to stay within a healthy weight range. Her boyfriend, Daniel, has just proposed, but Annie is scared stiff of marrying him. All his siblings and most of their children are obese. From Annie's viewpoint, the family has an unhealthy relationship with food. Annie feared her children would be doomed to obesity.

Unlike his siblings, Daniel maintains a healthy weight and exercises regularly. However, he snacks often and loves to eat out. He finds great delight in sharing tasty treats with Annie, and she has gained a few pounds since she started dating him over a year ago. Annie believes any meal consisting of more than protein (chicken or fish) and green salad or fruit sabotages her diet and puts her at risk of obesity. Her dread of gaining weight keeps her in a state of anxiety and often puts a damper on her and Daniel's fun.

Fear Analysis

The fear of gaining weight is rooted in the core fears of *inadequacy*, *losing control*, and *loneliness*. The *extreme* fear of weight gain is manifested in two eating disorders: anorexia nervosa, in which people purposefully starve themselves, and bulimia, in which people secretly binge on food and then purge by vomiting, using laxatives, fasting, or exercising excessively. According to news reports, Christy Henrich suffered from both disorders.

People who battle these conditions have a distorted body image and believe they weigh too much or look too heavy regardless of their actual weight or appearance. Eating disorders are more common in people who engage in sports or professions that prize thinness (e.g., dancers, figure skaters, gymnasts, models, and actors). Of course, college students competing for dates and people from families that place a high value on appearance are also at risk.

While there is no single root cause of anorexia or bulimia, research suggests that sufferers are generally affected by one or more factors, including genetic predisposition, chemical imbalance, traumatic events (e.g., sexual, physical, or emotional abuse), family dysfunction, and sensitivity to media messages about the ideal body. Other causes include fear of rejection by a spouse or romantic partner and an effort to cope with problems when one feels out of control.

The National Institute of Mental Health (NIMH) estimates that 0.6 percent of the adult population in the U.S. will suffer from anorexia, 1.0 percent from bulimia, and 2.8 percent from a binge eating disorder. The incidence of male eating disorders accounts for less than 10 percent of reported cases, but it is on the increase.[3]

There is hope. The phenomenal success of Dove Corporation's "Campaign for Real Beauty" indicates that many women are pushing back at the beauty industry's emphasis on physical perfection. Launched in 2004, the print ads for the company's firming lotion featured women of different shapes in sizes 12-14. The women appeared to have thrown off their insecurities, gotten comfortable in their own skin, and abandoned their pursuit of unattainable images of beauty.

In spite of this, Brigham Young University researchers used MRI technology to observe what happened in the brain when people viewed images of female strangers who were overweight. They found that the image activated an area in women's brains that processes identity and self-reflection. Men did not show signs of any self-reflection in similar situations. "These women have no history of eating disorders and project an attitude that they don't care about body image," said Mark Allen, a BYU neuroscientist. "Yet under the surface is an anxiety about getting fat and the centrality of body image to self."[4]

Action Plan

The fear of gaining weight is a mental disorder that dies hard. Try these suggestions to get on the road to healing:

- Remember that your body is not your own: "Do you not know that your body is the temple of the Holy Spirit who is in you, whom you have from God, and you are not your own? For you were bought at a price; therefore glorify God in your body and in your spirit, which are God's" (1 Corinthians 6:19-20). Step outside yourself mentally and understand that you are a steward or manager of the body God has entrusted to you to do His will here on earth.

- Keep a food journal to determine how much you are eating or *not* eating. Focus on eating foods that *bless* your body, such as protein, complex carbohydrates (fruit, vegetables, and whole grains), unsaturated fats, and so forth. Avoid or minimize foods that *curse* your body, such as refined carbohydrates (e.g., cookies, cakes, pies), saturated fats, and high-sodium items.

- Listen to the warnings and concerns of loved ones, friends, or coworkers about your unhealthy weight. Check your weight against standard height and weight charts to see if you are at a significant variation.

- Get professional help. Don't try to conquer this fear alone. Most people who suffer extreme fear of gaining weight are blind to the physical or psychological havoc they are wreaking on their bodies. Therefore, you must solicit or accept the assistance of others in establishing a qualified "professional survival team," which may include a medical doctor, nutritionist, and psychiatrist. *Note to family members:* Intervene quickly if you see signs of an eating disorder; don't wait for your loved one to see the problem.

- Avoid or minimize social interaction with critical, fat-phobic people with a judgmental attitude toward those who are overweight. They are masking their own insecurities and reinforcing your distorted self-image.

- Be patient and stay the course. You may have several ups and downs, but with commitment and determination, you will get on the road to freedom. Daily affirm, "Today I will manage God's body for His glory."

Day 22

Fear of Aging

The fear of the LORD adds length to life,
but the years of the wicked are cut short.
PROVERBS 10:27 NIV

Anita Bogan died in 2007 at the ripe old age of 106. Her obituary in the March 17, 2007 *Los Angeles Times* gave us a peek at a woman who enjoyed life:

> Blessed with good health and a sound mind, Bogan spent most of her old age doing what she wanted to do, with a feisty, "what's-age-got-to-do-with-it" attitude. In the decades following her 80th year, she created a non-profit foundation to build senior housing, made frequent trips to Las Vegas… opened a floral shop…played golf daily…took cruises to celebrate her birthdays…and inspired people.

On her 100th birthday, the Kern County Board of Supervisors declared an "Anita Bogan Day." Simply by living, Anita changed the way those around her thought about aging.

Caleb, the eighty-five-year-old Israelite leader, survived

the forty-year trek though the wilderness. He and Joshua were the only leaders left of the twelve Moses sent to spy out the Promised Land (see Numbers 13–14). God had destroyed the remaining ten because of their unbelief, along with all the Israelites twenty years old and older. Caleb arrived at his long-awaited destination full of fire and faith—ready to conquer his mountain (still inhabited by giants known as Anakim) and totally persuaded that God would help him do so.

> *"As yet I am as strong this day as on the day that Moses sent me; just as my strength was then, so now is my strength for war, both for going out and for coming in. Now therefore, give me this mountain of which the Lord spoke in that day; for you heard in that day how the Anakim were there, and that the cities were great and fortified. It may be that the Lord will be with me, and I shall be able to drive them out as the Lord said"* (JOSHUA 14:11-12).

Anita Bogan and Caleb proved that old age does not have to be the curse conventional wisdom makes it out to be.

Fear Analysis

Gerontophobia, the fear of aging, is rooted in the core fears of *pain and death*, *loneliness*, *inadequacy*, *losing control*, and for many, the fear of *lack*. With so many aspects of life at risk, it's no wonder that old age is such a dreaded phase.

The aging of the population of the United States is a widely reported phenomenon. Persons sixty-five years old and older numbered 39.6 million in 2009 and represented 12.9 percent of the population, about one in every eight Americans. By 2030, there will be about 72.1 million older persons representing 19 percent of the population (almost one in every five Americans).[5] This has significant implications for the nation's health, social, and economic institutions. It also causes anxiety for those struggling to hold on to their youth.

Action Plan

Someone once said, "Age is an issue of mind over matter. If you don't mind, it doesn't matter!" Try the suggestions below to help you change your perspective and begin to embrace aging as a gift.

- Strengthen your connection with your Creator. Read a passage of Scripture daily and meditate on God's faithfulness. Get to know the One with whom you will spend eternity.

- Come to grips with the reality of aging. You have been aging from the moment you were conceived. In fact, on the day of your birth, you were already nine months old, assuming your mother carried you to full term. You are aging every second. Therefore, fretting about getting older is as fruitless as worrying about the sun going down each day; it is inevitable and uncontrollable. The wise person simply makes plans to enjoy the morning, noon, and sunset. He plans to maximize every stage of his existence.

- Guard your health. Studies show that good health is the number one factor in determining the level of happiness in old age. Eat healthy and exercise often. Occasional indulgences are part of living, so give yourself permission to break the rules sometimes. Drink lots of water, take your daily vitamins, and get regular medical checkups. These efforts will not guarantee you *more* time, but they will influence the *quality* of your time here on earth.

- Dress as stylishly at every age as your budget will allow. When you look good, you feel good—and inspired. *Caution:* Keep your quest for attractiveness in balance. Think twice and do your homework before you submit to cosmetic surgeries. Some can be downright dangerous. "Charm is deceitful and beauty is passing, but a woman who fears the LORD, she shall be praised" (Proverbs 31:30).

- Always have a mountain to conquer, a goal to achieve. It doesn't have to be something big in the eyes of the world, just something to look forward to doing with your hands and your mind. Eleanor Roosevelt once said, "I could not, at any age, be content to take my place in a corner by the fireside and simply look on." Projects give purpose and direction. My friend Esther Eutsey, who is over eighty-six years old, still enrolls in classes ranging from computers to money management. She also works as an official caregiver to people significantly younger.

- Socialize with younger and older people to keep a balanced perspective on life.

- Keep your intellect sharp by reading a variety of books from different genres and by working crossword puzzles and similar activities that engage your thinking.

- Work on a legacy of service. Mother Teresa of Calcutta used to say, "The world is hungry for our help and our love." You will reap the benefits of the service you render to others.

- Rather than obsessing about the good old days, seek ways to make new memories. Occasionally celebrate holidays in different ways, in different places, and with different people.

- Make every effort to maintain a great attitude; it's a people magnet. A negative or critical spirit repels.

- Get your financial house in order. Identify a trustworthy person to be the executor of your will or hold power of attorney over your financial and medical wishes. If you can afford it, get long-term care insurance years before you'll need it so that you can remain in your home or afford a quality nursing facility in your later years. If you fear poverty, seek financial counseling to determine what key decisions you need to make now to maintain a quality life in old age. Read chapter 30 on "Fear of Retiring Poor" for additional financial strategies.

• Meditate on Scripture that exalts aging, such as Psalm 92:13-14:

*Those who are planted in the house
  of the LORD
Shall flourish in the courts of our God.
They shall still bear fruit in old age;
They shall be fresh and flourishing.*

Day 23

Fear of Helplessness
or Losing Control

"And now, Lord, what do I wait for?
My hope is in You."

PSALM 39:7

Barbara's doctor just delivered the news she's always dreaded—she has inoperable cancer.

Marge's rebellious twenty-two-year-old son is addicted to drugs.

Sally's verbally abusive husband is bipolar but refuses to seek help.

Ruben and his wife, Gail, lost their jobs in the same week; they have no cash reserves.

Fifty-year-old Erica, who comes from a family plagued by mental illness, has been hearing voices, but tries to ignore them for fear she's having a nervous breakdown.

Reverend Jim and his family got stuck on the interstate highway while trying to evacuate their coastal city before the hurricane hit. They were able to advance only one mile in two hours.

Job, overwhelmed with physical and emotional suffering, exclaimed,

> *"I don't have the strength to endure.*
> *I have nothing to live for...*
> *No, I am utterly helpless,*
> *without any chance of success."*
>
> (JOB 6:11,13 NLT)

Once God intervened in Job's situation, this upright man changed his attitude.

These scenarios of our inability to control our circumstances can cause great anxiety. Unfortunately, everyone will experience some form of helplessness at some point.

Fear Analysis

Fear of *helplessness* or *losing control* is one of the five core fears that forms the bedrock of many other fears discussed in this book. No study or poll could ever measure the prevalence of this fear; it affects every social and economic level of society.

Many of us struggle with control. We want control not only over our circumstances, but our goals and plans, relationships, and all that concerns us. Such fear is often an indication of an unconscious desire to be independent of God, to be the master of our destiny. It is often the result of growing up in a chaotic environment and resolving never to repeat the experience in your own life.

This is what made me fear losing control. I observed my mother's powerlessness because of her lack of education or financial options beyond my dad's support.

Therefore, I purposed never to be dependent on anyone for financial support, never to fall in love too deeply, and to avoid lack by always having adequate life, medical, auto, disability, or other insurance. While some of my actions were practical, my core motive was to be self-reliant. Suffice to say, life's circumstances and good mentoring corrected a lot of my flawed thinking.

Perhaps you foolishly believe you have controlled your life because of your academic, financial, political, or other achievements. It's a myth. God enabled you to do all that you have done. Thus, it would be fitting to regularly affirm the words of the apostle Paul: "But whatever I am now, it is all because God poured out his special favor on me—and not without results. For I have worked harder than any of the other apostles; yet it was not I but God who was working through me by his grace" (1 Corinthians 15:10 NLT).

Action Plan

If you find yourself trying to control every aspect of your life and striving to avoid any potential helplessness, try these strategies for developing the right mindset:

- Understand you are not an independent, self-sufficient being. You belong to God: "We are His people and the sheep of His pasture" (Psalm 100:3). Ask for grace to leave the shepherding of your life to your Father. Your mandate is simply to acknowledge Him and heed His direction.

- Practice responding calmly to unexpected occurrences (such as freeway traffic jams, electrical blackouts, and unannounced guests). Remember that God is not ever surprised and has a purpose for everything.

- Strive to maintain an *internal* versus an *external* focus in every situation. Once you settle within yourself that you cannot control any external happenings but only your internal response, you'll stop stressing over the uncontrollable or the inevitable. For example, when you encounter a nasty clerk, don't retaliate. Take a deep breath (to slow the flow of adrenaline), and send up a silent prayer for her. Then, if you can do it calmly, you may wish to address her behavior.

- Be spontaneous and refrain from controlling every detail of your vacations or other activities. I know a couple who goes on vacation and buys their clothes once they arrive at their destination rather than packing them from home. Too risky for me!

- Rather than dreading helplessness, embrace it as a place of strength. It positions you to experience God's power. "My grace is sufficient for you, for My strength is made perfect in weakness" (2 Corinthians 12:9).

- Be quick to express your helplessness to God.

King Jehoshaphat provides a great model. Realizing that his army was no match for three invading armies, he exclaimed, "O our God…we have no power against this great multitude that is coming against us; nor do we know what to do, but our eyes are upon You" (2 Chronicles 20:12). This miraculous story ends with the invading armies destroying each other. Jehoshaphat's army did not have to fight at all. Your biggest miracles will often happen when you feel the least empowered or the most vulnerable. God already knows that apart from Him, you can do *nothing* (John 15:5).

- Meditate on Scriptures that speak to the sovereignty of God and the futility of trying to control your life. Try these for starters:

We may throw the dice,
  but the LORD determines how they fall.

  (PROVERBS 16:33 NLT)

You can make many plans,
  but the LORD's purpose will prevail.

  (PROVERBS 19:21 NLT)

"All the people of the earth
  are nothing compared to him.
He does as he pleases
  among the angels of heaven
  and among the people of the earth.

No one can stop him or say to him,
'What do you mean by doing these things.'"

(DANIEL 4:35 NLT)

You saw me before I was born.
Every day of my life was recorded in your book.
Every moment was laid out
before a single day had passed.

(PSALM 139:16 NLT)

Day 24

Fear of Change
and Letting Go

*"Change is the law of life. And those
who look only to the past or present
are certain to miss the future."*

JOHN F. KENNEDY,
THIRTY-FIFTH PRESIDENT OF THE UNITED STATES

"Leave your native country, your relatives, and your father's family, and go to the land that I will show you" (Genesis 12:1 NLT). God's vague instructions to seventy-five-year-old Abraham and his sixty-five-year-old barren wife, Sarah, must have come as a great shock. Why did He ask these senior citizens to uproot their lives and move to some unknown destination? Because He had a divine destiny for them! He promised, "I will make you into a great nation. I will bless you and make you famous, and you will be a blessing to others" (Genesis 12:2 NLT). With no hint of resistance, Abraham embraced the change, trusted God, and eventually reaped the rewards—which included innumerable descendants. It's no wonder history calls him the Father of Faith.

Like death and taxes, change is inevitable. Most people resist it. I resisted it when God called me away from my job as the chief financial officer of a mega-church that I loved and the best boss imaginable. My new assignment was to pursue a full-time writing and speaking career. My job had paid well; the new undertaking would be an adventure in faith. I had visions of speaking to small groups or small churches and receiving a fruit basket as an honorarium. After all, it had happened once (amazing how we can allow one incident to color our expectations). While ministry to others is indeed my primary motivation, consistent results such as this would surely wreak havoc on our monthly budget. Notwithstanding, I overcame the fear of change and took the plunge. Today, I can say without a doubt that God "is able to do exceedingly abundantly above all that we ask or think" (Ephesians 3:20).

Fear Analysis

The fear of change has its roots in several core fears depending on the nature of the change: fear of *losing control*, fear of *lack*, fear of *inadequacy*, and fear of *loneliness*. As with all fears, the fear of change focuses on the future, the unknown. Consider this list of changes you may be resisting:

- Leaving an unfulfilling or low-paying job

- Starting a business

- Letting go of an unprofitable business

- Upgrading your computer and other electronic equipment

- Abandoning a toxic or ungodly relationship

- Getting rid of clothes not worn in years

- Letting go of an unaffordable home, auto, or lifestyle

- Establishing and adhering to a responsible spending plan

All of the above represent changes you would make voluntarily. However, panic can set in if the change is *unexpected*. Our response to unexpected changes is a test of our belief that "all things work together for good to those who love God" (Romans 8:28).

We all would like to be in control of our lives; unfortunately, being in control is a myth. The pace of life is just too dizzying to handle with our natural abilities. In the final analysis, you will overcome the fear of change only by surrendering your will to God, embracing the changes He permits, and casting all your care upon Him.

Action Plan

Those who can flow with change tend to be less stressed and generally happier. Try these solutions for embracing change and "letting go and letting God" do His thing in your life:

- Start developing a "change mindset" by doing

even routine things differently (sit in a different section at church, take an alternate route to work, and so on). Ask friends and family to point out areas where you consistently demonstrate inflexibility.

• When confronted with a dreaded or unexpected change, take authority over the spirit of fear. As a born-again believer, you can boldly pray: *Father, I thank You that You have given me authority over all the power of the enemy (Luke 10:19). Therefore, I cast my concern and fears regarding this change upon You now. I surrender to Your plan for my life. In the name of Jesus, I pray. Amen.*

• Ponder the benefits of the change rather than the temporary discomfort or inconvenience. Be honest with yourself about what you really fear about the change. Tell God about it.

• Keep an open attitude to new ideas and processes. Don't chime in with or be influenced by rigid thinkers.

• Establish "islands of stability" in your daily life. Alvin Toffler, author of *Future Shock,* asserted that people living in times of rapid change need what he called "islands of stability"—things that do not change. These activities keep you anchored to what's really important. For me, this includes attending weekly church service, being faithful to Date Night with my husband, visiting my mother, celebrating key family and friends' birthdays, making a weekly call to my elderly aunt who lives out of state, and chatting with any one of my seven brothers. I suggest that you too establish or remain faithful to your "islands of stability."

Day 25

Fear of Failure

*"Success is the ability to go from failure to
failure without losing your enthusiasm."*
WINSTON CHURCHILL

The following summary, highlighting the period of
Abraham Lincoln's life from 1831–1860, appears under a
popular portrait of him:

> He failed in business in '31. He was defeated for
> state legislator in '32. He tried another business in
> '33. It failed. His fiancée died in '35. He had a ner-
> vous breakdown in '36. In '43 he ran for Congress and
> was defeated. He tried again in '48 and was defeated
> again. He tried running for the Senate in '55. He lost.
> The next year he ran for Vice President and lost. In '59
> he ran for the Senate again and was defeated. In 1860,
> the man who signed his name A. Lincoln was elected
> the 16th President of the United States. The differ-
> ence between history's boldest accomplishments and
> its most staggering failures is often, simply, the dili-
> gent will to persevere.[6]

Here was a man who refused to allow fear of failure

to block his progress. Throughout history and the Bible, we find that all great people failed in some way. What about you? Have past failures or the thought of future failure stopped you from starting a business, teaching a Bible study, writing a book, pursuing a course of study?

Fear Analysis

Fear of failure is rooted in the core fear of *inadequacy*. This fear is based on the erroneous belief that the success of our undertakings rests solely on our efforts and abilities. And because we are keenly aware of our human limitations, we limit our pursuits to our comfort zone. This can lead to a life of unfulfilled dreams and frustration about what "could have been."

As I sit here typing, I marvel at how reluctant I was to write my first book. Even though it was only sixty-four pages long, it was way out of my comfort zone as a CPA. I had limited my professional activities to preparation and presentation of financial statements and analyses. I never dreamed that God would use such an inexperienced vessel to influence lives around the world. Just today, I received an email from a counselor in India expressing gratitude for one of my books; it was humbling and rewarding to read.

We must realize that we can never please God and be all that He wants us to be if we live within a realm that doesn't require us to exercise our faith. "But without faith it is impossible to please Him" (Hebrews 11:6). I have observed that the more unfamiliar a person is with God's promises and His workings in the affairs of ordinary men and women as revealed in the Scriptures, the more likely that person is to fear failure. Many often conclude that a task is impossible without stopping to realize that Jesus is still saying to His followers, "Did I not say to you that if you would believe you would see the glory of God" (John 11:40)?

Action Plan

Consider the strategies below for overcoming your fear of failure and moving toward the results you desire:

- Make sure your pursuits reflect your true aspirations. Nothing could be worse than climbing the ladder to success and discovering when you reach the top that it was leaning on the wrong building. I once worked with a spacecraft engineer who revealed he had graduated from medical school only to find that he had no passion for the profession. He had wasted all those years to placate the desires of his well-meaning parents. Lack of passion for your pursuit will surely lead to failure.

- Define success based on your core values versus those of an ego-driven, success-mad world. Being publically recognized and applauded for your achievements while your family life is in shambles is not success. For me as an author and speaker, I refuse to define success as a totally booked speaking calendar and loads of media appearances. Rather, I value a balanced life that includes a fulfilling marriage, quality time (although scheduled) with family and friends, and the knowledge that I'm doing exactly what God has called me to do.

- Quiz your doubts. Ask yourself, "What is the worst that can happen if I don't succeed? Will my family desert me? Will I be punished legally? Has this *ever* been done before (even if not, so what)? Is this fear a signal that I don't have the proper people, processes, or plans in place to succeed at this time?" Then, ask the really big question: "What are the prime benefits I'll enjoy if I succeed?"

- Maintain a can-do attitude. Boldly assert, "I can do all things through Christ who strengthens me" (Philippians 4:13). Don't let the familiarity of this passage cause you to recite it by rote. Really absorb the words; get them into your spirit. Know that Christ *strengthens* you to succeed for the glory of God. Where He guides, He provides all the resources needed.

- Determine to learn from failure and mistakes. Failure is not fatal and neither does it define who you are. It is simply the results of your actions, not a measure of your worthiness. Thomas Edison once said, "I have not failed. I've just found 10,000 ways that won't work."

- Just do it, even if for only a short time. Perhaps you read the story of Peter's attempt to walk on the water and judged him a failure (see Matthew 14:22-33). I beg to differ. First, Peter gets an *A* for getting out of the boat. Second, he experienced the exhilaration of actually walking on the water even if for only a fleeting moment; no other disciple could boast that. Third, he learned a valuable lesson: Focusing on Jesus rather than the circumstances is essential when attempting the impossible. Fourth, he recognized that his survival depended solely on Jesus. When Peter saw he was "beginning to sink he cried out, saying, 'Lord, save me!' And immediately Jesus stretched out His hand and caught him" (Matthew 14:30-31). Peter did not rely on his swimming skills to get to safety. Know this, Jesus will catch you and assure your survival in your endeavors when you call upon Him.

Part 4

Financial Fears

Day 26

Fear of Success

*"Your belief determines your action
and your action determines your
results, but first you have to believe."*

MARK VICTOR HANSEN, COAUTHOR OF
THE CHICKEN SOUP FOR THE SOUL SERIES

Researchers conducted an experiment in which several frogs were each placed in separate glass jars covered with a lid to prevent them from escaping. They were given food, air, and water. At first, the frogs kept jumping, trying to escape, but each time they would hit their head on the lid.

After thirty days, the researchers removed the lids. Although the lids were no longer present, the frogs never jumped out of the jars, even though they could have easily done so. During the thirty days of their captivity, the frogs learned they could not escape. They formed a belief that the top of the jar was as high as they could go. Even when the lid was removed, their limiting belief kept them where they were.

This simple experiment demonstrates the power of a belief system. Many of us still hold on to limiting beliefs even though they are no longer true and are limiting our true potential.[1]

Many women, minorities, and other frequently disadvantaged groups have accepted the idea of the corporate glass ceiling (limited advancement due to discrimination) and settled into mediocre positions despite the strides others have made over the past decades. What they do not realize is that many companies have taken the lid off the jar and are objectively seeking talented managers to achieve corporate goals.

Fear Analysis

Opposite the fear of *failure*, the fear of *success* stems from several limiting beliefs:

- fear of the inadequacy to maintain the success

- fear of the inability to meet the expectations and responsibility that accompany success

- fear of rejection and alienation by those unhappy about your success

- fear of losing control of normal, private life

- fear of saying no to friends and family who feel entitled to your wealth

Further, some people fear success because of their erroneous belief that they are not worthy of abundance or anything beyond the ordinary. Whatever the root cause, it seems odd that anyone would fear success since successful people tend to travel, drive fancy cars, dine in fancy restaurants, get preferential treatment in almost all venues of life, give to charity, and obtain all the external trappings of "happiness."

Fear of success is characterized by self-sabotaging behaviors such as procrastinating, underperforming, pretending not to know to avoid rejection, allowing yourself to be sidetracked by so many insignificant things that you never get focused on the main thing, and always talking about what you plan to do "someday." Some of these actions are done subconsciously.

Action Plan

If you are ready to overcome the fear of success and position yourself to be a blessing to others, try these strategies:

- Consider whether you have a fear of success in light of the discussion above.

- Determine the source of any erroneous beliefs you may harbor regarding your unworthiness, such as rejection by loved ones, comparisons to others, and media images. Your perception of your worthiness will play a major role in how much you *allow* yourself to achieve in life.

- Recognize your self-sabotaging behavior and commit to putting a stop to it. This means abandoning procrastination and giving yourself ample time to complete critical tasks on which your success hinges. It also means guarding your "success-already-in-progress" and not engaging in actions that thwart it (for example, accumulating cash reserves for your small business, then spending the funds on clothes versus marketing and publicity). It also means timely follow-up with key individuals who can influence outcomes significant to your success.

I used to behave horribly in this area. I could meet the "President of the World" and never follow up, even though he had given me his personal contact information and asked me to do so. I would think, *Who am I to have such access? Where could this lead?* I felt unworthy of such favor—until I grasped the reality of Proverbs 22:29:

Do you see a man who excels in his work?
He will stand before kings;
He will not stand before unknown men.

Now I know it is God who brings us before people of great influence.

- Seek to associate with goal-oriented finishers who get things done and who demonstrate the right priorities in doing so. Watch how they operate and emulate the God-honoring aspect of their behavior.

- Consider the good you can do as a successful person. Think of the nonselfish actions you would take or charities, ministries, and causes you would support right now if you had wealth beyond your needs.

- Understand that success is God's idea, and He gives it to us for His purpose (Deuteronomy 8:18) and His glory. "Let the LORD be magnified, Who has pleasure in the prosperity of His servant" (Psalm 35:27).

Day 27

Fear of Lack

The LORD is my shepherd;
I shall not want.

PSALM 23:1

During a talk show interview, a popular Hollywood superstar was asked how it felt to have so much money at his disposal having grown up poor. He confessed that he still had much anxiety about experiencing lack in the future. Thus he tended to be frugal, viewed the money as somewhat surreal, and wasn't able to relax and fully embrace the wealth that had come with his success. However, his wife had brought balance to the relationship with a mindset of give, spend, and save. This couple's generosity is well-documented.

At the risk of sounding overconfident, I am fully persuaded that I'm never going to experience lack as long as the Lord is my shepherd. I believe with all my heart that I've ensured myself against lack by standing on God's promises and obeying specific commands, such as: "Give, and it will be given to you: good measure, pressed down, shaken together, and running over will be put into your bosom. For with the same measure that you use, it will be measured back to you" (Luke 6:38).

I live by this promise. And, though I have been a tither since 1968, my conviction of God's faithfulness in my finances has been tested many times over the years. However, each time I have been on the brink of lack, my Shepherd stepped in and provided. For example, the subsidiary where I worked many years ago at a Fortune 500 company was closed down. I had no job prospects, but my Shepherd was on His job. Another Fortune 500 company called and offered me a job at a 20 percent raise; they created the position for me after I came aboard.

In another instance many years ago, Darnell and I were trying to buy our dream house but needed to submit a down payment within five days—not enough time to close the sale of our current home and use the proceeds. The amount required was ten times more than we had available in cash. But God gave me favor with my employer, and I obtained a temporary, interest-free advance within forty-eight hours. I have a number of these adventures in faith stories—enough to convince me that my Shepherd is "able to do exceedingly abundantly above all that we ask or think" (Ephesians 3:20).

Fear Analysis

The fear of lack is a core fear that drives many other fears, including the fear of becoming disabled, fear of aging, fear of investing, and, the fear of retiring poor. Lack suggests that one is without or has less than a desirable quantity of something. The prospect of not having enough can be anxiety producing for the unbeliever, and often, the believer.

I believe the fear of lack is one of the root causes of greed. Some people get so obsessed with ensuring themselves against the possibility of not having enough that they go overboard. I have known people who have come from a disadvantaged background who spend every waking moment trying to make enough money so that neither they nor their kids ever have to experience the discomfort, inconvenience, and helplessness of lack. Like all fears, the fear of lack is based on an erroneous belief about God and His ability or willingness to handle the situation.

Action Plan

Our Shepherd never intended for us to assume ultimate responsibility for our lives nor to live as if His promises are of no effect. A good strategy is to *learn* the promises, *understand* the ones that are conditional, *meet* the condition, and *rest* in His love and faithfulness. This doesn't mean that we sit idly and wait for God to do what He has given us the ability to do. We must do the *natural* things and trust Him for the *super*natural. Start (or continue) to implement these practical strategies:

- Pay your tithes—10 percent of your "increase" (earnings and cash gifts). Don't debate whether it's an Old Testament mandate versus a New Testament requirement. I'd rather do more than required than find out later I fell short of God's expectations.

- Commit to a consistent savings plan. Aim for at least 5 percent of your income.

- Consider the areas of lack you fear the most such as shelter or food. Which of these do you erroneously believe God is incapable of providing? Now, cast down those imaginations and replace them with this promise: "God will generously provide all you need. Then you will always have everything you need and plenty left over to share with others" (2 Corinthians 9:8 NLT).

- Refuse to put your faith in your credentials, marketable skills, or influential contacts for assurance of financial provision.

- Give beyond your tithes to those in need. In so doing, you will create a valuable asset— an IOU from God. "He who has pity on the poor lends to the LORD, and He will pay back what he has given" (Proverbs 19:17).

Fear of Losing a Job

*A prudent person foresees danger
and takes precautions.
The simpleton goes blindly on
and suffers the consequences.*
PROVERBS 22:3 NLT

Joan has heard rumors of cutbacks and senses that she is in danger of losing her job. For the past few weeks, everybody else at the company has been putting in long hours while she is relegated to insignificant tasks. Even after she requested to work on a project, her boss ignored her. Joan is getting panicky because she is a single parent who lives from paycheck to paycheck. She also has a sickly three-year-old who requires frequent doctor visits. Without the company's medical coverage, he will not get proper care.

Joan's attempt to balance her finances with her current economic realities has taken a toll on her physically and emotionally. She gets very little sleep each night because she is also pursuing website development as a sideline business. Her client base is steadily growing. Her fatigue causes her to be a little cranky with the other employees. She also takes off more sick days than the others. Each morning she comes to work, she worries, *Is this the day I get the ax?*

The truth is that Joan hates her job. Her supervisor is obnoxious and inept. Further, Joan has no real interest or passion for the widgets the company produces. She has daydreamed for the past two years of pursuing the website development business full-time; however, most of her clients are referred by friends, and she offers her service at deeply discounted rates. So for now, she has opted to settle for the false security of a regular paycheck.

Fear Analysis

The fear of losing a job is common, especially during uncertain economic times. The U.S. Bureau of Labor Statistics reported that over eight million jobs were lost from December 2007 to December 2010 while the national unemployment rate hovered around 9.7 percent (approximately fifteen million workers) of the American working population. With statistics like these, it's easy to see why so many people live in fear of becoming unemployed.

The fear of losing a job is rooted in the core fears of *lack* ("How will I meet my obligations?"), *inadequacy* ("I'm not good enough"), *helplessness or losing control* ("What do I do now?"), and *loneliness* ("I'll be isolated from my social network"). For some, the shame and humiliation of losing a job are as devastating as the loss of income.

Fretting about being fired can become a self-fulfilling prophecy as the anxiety makes you more ineffective.

Action Plan

If you live in fear of unemployment, it's time to stop worrying and start developing a strategy that will enhance your position on the job or assure a soft landing if you do get the boot. Try these moves now:

- Endeavor to be as indispensable as possible. Strive for excellence in your work while learning as much as possible about procedures and processes beyond your area of responsibility. Be willing to help others—but not at the expense of your own effectiveness. Stay balanced here.

- If the fear of losing your job stems from personality clashes with your boss, decide to embrace the biblical principle of authority and submission. The buck stops with the person in charge—without regard to gender. Therefore, determine to submit and say OK to anything asked of you that is not illegal or immoral. Just be wise and confirm the instructions from your boss with a follow-up memo, including your feedback on the potential outcome. Watch your tone so that it doesn't sound as if you're trying to cover yourself; no need to copy higher ups for now. Getting along with your boss is crucial, so make doing so your special project.

- Assess your marketability. Are you in a field with strong demand for your skills or do you need to take a short course to upgrade them? Be willing to invest the time to do what's necessary.

- Increase your visibility in your industry. Establish contacts and relationships with others outside your company by attending local industry gatherings wherever possible. God will surround you with favor as He sees fit: "For You, O LORD, will bless the righteous; with favor You will surround him as with a shield" (Psalm 5:12).

- Pare your personal expenses to the bare minimum. You may need to consider a less expensive mode of transportation, take your lunch, and use other cost-saving measures.

- Accumulate as large a cash reserve as possible (three- to six-months' living expenses). Remember you are not putting your faith in the reserve; you are simply foreseeing the danger and taking precautions. Knowing that you've been financially responsible will ease some of your anxiety.

- Maintain a divine perspective on your job. Remind yourself that it is not your *source*, but a *chosen channel* of God's provision for a *chosen season*. Read the story of Elijah the prophet and how God miraculously provided for him through a raven, a brook, and a starving single parent (1 Kings 17).

- Take the stigma out of being fired or laid off. Why assume that people will think it was your fault or that you are now inferior in some way? People will generally respond to your situation the same way that you do. They will find your enthusiasm about your next move inspiring—even though you may not yet know what it is. When you serve God, there is a good purpose associated with everything that happens to you (Romans 8:28). For many, being fired was the kick start they needed to enter the world of entrepreneurship.

- Remember the two abiding truths: your destiny is in God's hands and He "shall supply all your need according to His riches in glory by Christ Jesus" (Philippians 4:19). So renounce that spirit of fear!

Day 29

Fear of Investing or Losing Money

"The greatest cause of human financial struggle is the fear of losing money."
ROBERT KIYOSAKI

The investment promoter's pitch sounded too good to be true, but a couple of high-profile celebrities had already invested in the company and their presence at the meeting added credibility. Of course, the 10 percent guaranteed *monthly* return sounded a little farfetched (that's a 120 percent profit in one year!), but there were people in the audience who had already earned such returns and were flashing copies of their cancelled checks to prove it. Besides, Mr. X, the company's president, promised a complete refund to any investor who wanted his principal back at the end of any month. But the mega return was available only to folks who left their money in the company.

So, with minimal due diligence, Darnell and I, two seasoned financial professionals, took the plunge.

Perhaps I should say "the fall." We actually reaped the promised profits during our first two months in the deal. However, in the third month, the whole scheme fell apart as the company was unable to recruit enough new investors to keep up with the promised payouts. Only the initial investors recouped 100 percent of their funds since they had earned such whopping profits over a longer period. Mr. X and a few of his cohorts were sentenced to prison, and we relearned an old lesson about investing and spending: "If it sounds too good to be true, it probably is." Our goal was simply to maximize the return on our cash rather than having it sit in low- to no-interest bearing bank accounts.

I'm sure that when investment phobic people hear a story like this, they make an even greater resolve to settle for low returns and avoid all transactions that carry any element of risk.

Interestingly, Jesus sanctioned the idea of maximizing the return on our investments. In Matthew 25:14-29, He relates a parable about a man who entrusted three different sums of money ("talents") to three of his servants to invest on his behalf while he went away on an extended trip. When he returned, he asked for an accounting of the funds. The two men he had given five talents and two talents to doubled their investment. The master commended them on their shrewd trading and rewarded them. However, the servant entrusted with one talent was so afraid of losing the money, he simply buried it in the ground to preserve the principal. The master was furious that he had behaved so foolishly and had robbed him of the opportunity to earn a profit. He called him "wicked and lazy" (verse 26).

The master knew what most loss-averse people don't: When money sits idly for a long period during inflationary times, it loses purchasing power. Ideally, idle funds should earn a rate of return that exceeds the inflation rate. If inflation is running at 3 percent but the interest rate on your savings is only 0.5 percent, you are losing 2.5 percent in purchasing power (before consideration of income taxes). Thus, the fear of investing in something with a little more risk but a higher rate of return can actually cause the very loss that you dread.

Fear Analysis

The fear of losing money is rooted in the core fears of *lack*, *losing control*, and *inadequacy*. As a CPA, I felt inadequate and embarrassed when our investment went bust. Moreover, I had worked for many years as a venture capitalist and had performed many due diligence reviews. We were simply too busy and distracted with other priorities. I felt angry and helpless as I followed news reports of the fraudulent company, its founder, and his fate.

Some scientists assert that our fear of losing money may be wired into our brains. Researchers at the California Institute of Technology studied a phenomenon known as "loss aversion" in two patients with lesions to the amygdala, a region deep within the brain involved in emotions and decision-making. "A fully-functioning amygdala appears to make us more cautious," explains Ralph Adolphs, professor of psychology and neuroscience.

"We already know that the amygdala is involved in processing fear, and it also appears to make us 'afraid' to risk losing money."[2]

Action Plan

As I've said throughout this book, we fear what we do not understand. Overcoming your fear of investing can be a simple, but not easy, process:

- *Get savvy.* Before you start investing outside your comfort zone, you need to learn the language and nuances of the stock market, real estate, mutual funds, and other transactions. A wealth of information is available on the Internet. Obviously, you'll have to learn how to use the computer to navigate your way to various financial websites, such as the American Association of Individual Investors (www.aaii .com), real estate investment (www.realestate investment101.info), and other user-friendly sites designed to enhance your investment knowledge.

  Further, numerous nonprofit organizations offer classes on the basics of investing. Yes, savings accounts, certificates of deposit, and money market accounts are great ways to protect your money while earning a modicum of interest. However, to make the highest return on your investment, you have to take on some risk, and the higher the risk, the greater the potential reward.

- *Get counsel.* Once you have a basic understanding of the lingo and the conventional wisdom of investing, it's time to get counsel for your specific situation. A certified public accountant, financial planner, or other personal finance expert will help you determine an asset allocation plan based upon your age and investment objectives. Talk to friends and relatives who have made investments; learn from their experiences. "Where there is no counsel, the people fall; but in the multitude of counselors there is safety" (Proverbs 11:14).

  Be wary of any expert who gets a commission from the investments he recommends; a fee-only arrangement is better. Most importantly, get the counsel of the Holy Spirit. If after you've prayed you still have some apprehensions about a recommended investment, don't be pressured to proceed. It's *your* money to *manage* for the glory of God.

- *Get moving.* Time is money. You'll go broke trying to save for big things like your kids' college education or your retirement if you don't take advantage of the high returns offered by the stock market and other investments over an extended period. Now, before you hand over your funds to a money manager, review the Securities and Exchange Commission's checklist (www.sec.gov/investor/pubs/invad visers.htm) for a summary of things to look for, questions to ask, and criteria for selecting an adviser.

Day 30

Fear of Retiring Poor

"Even to your old age, I am He,
And even to gray hairs I will carry you!"
Isaiah 46:4

Fifty-nine-year-old Annie had dreamed of early retirement at age sixty-two. However, the company where she worked for the past fifteen years downsized over two years ago, forcing her to take a lower-paying position or face unemployment. She promptly refinanced her home to adjust to her new economic realities.

Like three out of five baby boomers, Annie is financially unprepared to retire. Her golden years are looking bleak; her fear of retirement is running rampant. Annie has concluded she will have to depend on Social Security for a significant share of her retirement income. Unfortunately, the U.S. Social Security system is more broke than the people who need its benefits. A 2009 report from the Social Security and Medicare Boards of Trustees projected that the Social Security fund will be depleted by 2037 if reforms are not put in place.[3]

Thank God that He, rather than the government, is the source of all provision for His children. As someone once said, "God's retirement plan is out of this world!"

Fear Analysis

The fear of retiring broke is a rational fear—especially in uncertain economic times. It is rooted in the fear of *lack*, *inadequacy*, *losing control*, and *loneliness*. The prospect of retiring broke (or outliving savings and investments) after years of hard work can make one feel vulnerable. After all, work itself is a significant part of a lot of people's identity, especially men, who tend to evaluate their self-worth by their net worth. Further, many people are haunted by visions of homelessness, substandard nursing homes, and other woes of the poor and powerless. But there is hope.

Action Plan

Your strategy for overcoming retirement fears depends on how long you have to reach retirement age. Generally, you would be wise to do the following now:

- Find a financial planner to help you assess where you stand and the level of income and expenses you're likely to have during your retirement. She will customize a savings and investment plan suited to your financial goals. She will even estimate the number of years you can expect to live in retirement. (Relax— only God has that information.) The sooner you know what actions to take, the less confusion and anxiety you will experience.

- Get involved with a good church and be faithful to a small group (as well as social or community groups) who can get to know you and your retirement goals.

- Guard and nurture your relationship with your future support system (sons, daughters, their spouses, nieces, nephews, grandkids). This is no time to be cranky, super opinionated, or a pain in the neck. Become the type of person people want to embrace—and support. No, this is not a call to abandon who you are, but a challenge to be flexible, understanding, nonjudgmental, and amicable in your interactions with others.

- Intensify your efforts to stay physically and mentally fit so that you will be able to work well into your retirement years should you need to do so.

- Plan to put your experience and skills to good use by volunteering your time. This will not only be emotionally rewarding but will increase your social network of mutually beneficial relationships. Also, understand that Scripture does not support the American ideal of a carefree self-focused retirement. In fact, the Bible says very little about

retirement. Even when God set the retirement age at fifty for the priests' service in the
Tabernacle, He was very clear on their post-
retirement responsibilities: "they must retire
at the age of fifty. After retirement they may
assist their fellow Levites by serving as guards
at the Tabernacle, but they may not officiate
in the service. This is how you must assign
duties to the Levites" (Numbers 8:25-26 NLT).

Well, my friend, why should God keep
you around only to indulge your selfish
desires? Ask Him for a revelation of His
vision for your retirement.

- If you are near retirement, consider turning
  your hobbies into a part-time career even now.
  At a minimum, investigate what things must
  be in place to hit the ground running upon
  your retirement.

- If you own a home with substantial equity,
  investigate the merits of getting a reverse
  mortgage. This government-backed program is available only to those at least sixty-
  two years old. It can provide you with much
  needed cash flow and requires no monthly
  payments or qualifying income. See www
  .hud.gov/offices/hsg/sfh/hecm/hecmabou
  .cfm or contact your local lender for details.

- Plant seeds of generosity now by reaching out

in tangible ways to post-retirement age individuals. You will reap what you sow. (I assume that you are ensuring yourself against lack by obeying God in paying your tithes and giving offerings.)

• When tempted to fret about your future, meditate on Matthew 6:31-34 (NLT):

> *"So don't worry about these things, saying, 'What will we eat? What will we drink? What will we wear?' These things dominate the thoughts of unbelievers, but your heavenly Father already knows all your needs. Seek the Kingdom of God above all else, and live righteously, and he will give you everything you need.*
>
> *"So don't worry about tomorrow, for tomorrow will bring its own worries. Today's trouble is enough for today."*

Epilogue

Neutralize Your Fear…
Get Your Life in Gear

The first woman to win a Nobel Prize was French physicist and chemist Madame Marie Curie. She once said, "Nothing in life is to be feared, only understood." I pray that the brief discussions and practical challenges of the thirty common fears presented in this book have increased your understanding of them, given you hope, and inspired you to move from fear to peace through the powerful medium of your faith.

There are over two thousand phobias in the world today, and the list is growing; thus, we may not have addressed your particular fear. Rest assured that whether an anxiety, fear, or phobia, the power of God within you is stronger than anything you dread.

Throughout this book, I have tried to present you with strategies you can employ to overcome your fears. The following recommendations summarize what you can start doing today to get on the path to peace:

- Get the facts about the thing you fear; take the mystery and misinformation out of it.

- Put the fear in divine perspective. "Behold, I am the LORD, the God of all flesh. Is there anything too hard for Me?" (Jeremiah 32:27). Although you may believe God can indeed do anything, you must recognize the limiting beliefs you harbor about His *willingness* to do it for *you*.

- Relax. Envision yourself calm and free of the bondage of the fear. Consider the positive impact on your life once you are delivered.

- Confront each of your fear-triggering situations with baby steps. Every hurdle you overcome strengthens you to face the next one. Horatio Palmer, in the old hymn "Yield Not to Temptation," said it best: "Each vict'ry will help you some other to win."

In making these recommendations, I do not mean to imply that you may never need to seek outside support. If your anxiety has progressed to a phobia and you find yourself avoiding situations that trigger it, know that it's time to seek help. The wise counsel of Christian psychiatrists, psychologists, and other skilled professionals is invaluable. Your doctor may recommend drug therapy to suppress your fears. While it will not cure them, it may give you the clarity of mind to begin to address the root causes and to implement the needed behavioral changes.

Commit now to overcoming the fears that have wreaked havoc on your peace of mind.

Dear friend, Jesus has already provided for your peace. "Peace I leave with you, My peace I give to you; not as the world gives do I give to you. Let not your heart be troubled, neither let it be afraid" (John 14:27). The fact that Jesus used the word *let* indicates that the choice is yours and within your power. You must be proactive in arming yourself with the promises of God and running toward your fears.

Appendix 1 is a brief collection of general fear-fighting Scriptures that will strengthen your faith. Appendix 2 is a model of how to pray the promises and to make faith declarations that will bring peace to your soul. You can renounce the fears that are holding you back. You can "let the peace of God rule in your hearts."

Appendix 1

Fear-Fighting Scriptures

"Be strong and of good courage, and do it; do not fear nor be dismayed, for the LORD God—my God—will be with you. He will not leave you nor forsake you."

1 CHRONICLES 28:20

The LORD is my rock and my fortress and my deliverer;
My God, my strength, in whom I will trust;
My shield and the horn of my salvation, my stronghold.

PSALM 18:2

Yea, though I walk through the valley of the shadow of death, I will fear no evil;
For You are with me;
Your rod and Your staff, they comfort me.

PSALM 23:4

Whenever I am afraid,
I will trust in You.

PSALM 56:3

In God I have put my trust;
I will not be afraid.
What can man do to me?

PSALM 56:11

Surely he will never be shaken;
The righteous will be in everlasting remembrance.
He will not be afraid of evil tidings;
His heart is steadfast, trusting in the LORD.
His heart is established;
He will not be afraid.

PSALM 112:6-8

Do not be afraid of sudden terror,
Nor of trouble from the wicked when it comes;
For the LORD will be your confidence,
And will keep your foot from being caught.

PROVERBS 3:25-26

Behold, God is my salvation,
I will trust and not be afraid;
For YAH, the LORD, is my strength and song;
He also has become my salvation.

ISAIAH 12:2

"I, even I, am He who comforts you.
Who are you that you should be afraid
Of a man who will die,
And of the son of a man who will be made like grass?"

ISAIAH 51:12

"Peace I leave with you, My peace I give to you; not as the world gives do I give to you. Let not your heart be troubled, neither let it be afraid."

JOHN 14:27

Be anxious for nothing, but in everything by prayer and supplication, with thanksgiving, let your requests be made known to God; and the peace of God, which surpasses all understanding, will guard your hearts and minds through Christ Jesus.

PHILIPPIANS 4:6-7

Appendix 2

Fear-Banishing Prayer

Father, I enter into Your gates with thanksgiving and into Your courts with praise (Psalm 100:4). I am grateful to You for Your love, Your protection, and Your provision. I repent of every sin, failing, and shortcoming in my life that would hinder this prayer. I receive Your forgiveness now.

Father, the spirit of fear is trying to destroy my peace. I know that it did not come from You for You have given me a spirit of love, and of power, and a sound mind (2 Timothy 1:7). Therefore, I cast down every thought that is contrary to what Your Word says about You and Your power (2 Corinthians 10:5). Nothing is too hard for You (Jeremiah 32:27); You have the power to control every circumstance that comes my way (Daniel 4:35). I stand on Your promise that You will never leave me nor forsake me (Hebrews 13:5). As I seek Your face, I know You will hear me and deliver me from all my fears (Psalm 34:4).

Father, You are my refuge and my strength, a very present help in my time of trouble. Therefore, I will not fear (Psalm 46:1-2). Thank You in advance for working things out for Your glory and for my good according to Your divine plan and purpose (Romans 8:28). I boldly resist the spirit of fear now and command it to flee (James 4:7). Thank You that Your peace, which surpasses my understanding, is guarding my heart and my mind (Philippians 4:7). Therefore, I will not let my heart be troubled, neither will I let it be afraid (John 14:27). In the name of Jesus, I pray. Amen.

Notes

Part 1: Health and Safety Fears

1. www.personal-development.com/chuck/overcoming-fear-of-death.htm.
2. www.qohf.org/in_the_news.html.
3. www.disabilitycanhappen.org/chances_disability/default.asp.
4. www.aboutbugsbugsbugs.com/spiders/biology.htm.
5. www.nature.com/ncb/journal/v9/n9/full/ncb437.html.
6. www.austinlostpets.com/kidskorner/2october/pitbull.htm.
7. www.alainrobert.com.
8. www.crashstuff.com/driving-or-flying-plane-vs-car-accident-statistics/.
9. Keith Godfrey, *Flying Without Fear* (Hampshire, England: Macroteach Publications, 2003), 12.
10. www.conquerfear.com.
11. www.waterelementswim.com.
12. www.melondash.com.
13. http://ga.water.usgs.gov/edu/propertyyou.html.
14. www.brainyquote.com/quotes/quotes/v/virginiafo239011.html, accessed January 6, 2011.
15. For an in-depth look at how NCTC operates and what they are doing to ensure our safety, visit their website at www.nctc.gov.
16. www.fivethirtyeight.com/2009/12/odds-of-airborne-terror.html.

Part 2: Relational Fears

1. http://weeklywire.com/ww/12-07-98/alibi_facts.html.
2. www.leaderu.com/critical/cohabitation-socio.html.

Part 3: Psychological Fears

1. www.webmd.com/anxiety-panic/guide/20061101/fear-public
   -speaking.
2. www.worldlingo.com/ma/enwiki/en/Christy_Henrich.
3. To learn more about the causes, symptoms, and treatment of eating disorders, visit the NIMH website at www.nimh.nih.gov/health
   /topics/eating-disorders/index.shtml.
4. http://esciencenews.com/articles/2010/04/13/fear.getting.fat.seen
   .healthy.womens.brain.scans.
5. www.aoa.gov/aoaroot/aging_statistics/Census_Population/Index
   .aspx.
6. www.wemotivate.com/servlet/Detail?no=875.

Part 4: Financial Fears

1. www.eruptingmind.com/overcome-fear-of-success.
2. www.sciencedaily.com/releases/2010/02/100208154645.htm.
3. www.ssa.gov/OACT/TRSUM/index.html.

How to Contact the Author

Deborah Smith Pegues is a Bible teacher, a speaker, an experienced certified public accountant, a certified behavioral consultant specializing in understanding personality temperaments, and the author of *30 Days to Taming Your Tongue, 30 Days to Taming Your Stress, 30 Days to Taming Your Finances, Emergency Prayers,* and *Socially Smart in 60 Seconds.* She and her husband, Darnell, have been married since 1979 and make their home in California.

For speaking engagements, please contact the author at:

The Pegues Group
P.O. Box 56382
Los Angeles, California 90056
(323) 293-5861

or

E-mail: deborah@confrontingissues.com
www.confrontingissues.com

30 DAYS TO TAMING YOUR TONGUE
What You Say (and Don't Say) Will Improve Your Relationships

Certified behavioral consultant Deborah Smith Pegues knows how easily a slip of the tongue can cause problems in personal and business relationships. This is why she wrote the popular *30 Days to Taming Your Tongue* (280,000 copies sold). Now in trade size, Pegues' 30-day devotional will help each reader not only tame their tongue but make it productive rather than destructive.

With humor and a bit of refreshing sass, Deborah devotes chapters to learning how to overcome the

- Retaliating Tongue
- Know-It-All Tongue
- Belittling Tongue
- Hasty Tongue
- Gossiping Tongue
- 25 More!

Short stories, anecdotes, soul-searching questions, and scripturally based personal affirmations combine to make each applicable and life changing.

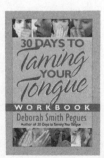

30 DAYS TO TAMING YOUR TONGUE WORKBOOK

If you're one of the thousands of readers who's found help in *30 Days to Taming Your Tongue*, this hands-on guide will help you keep on doing what you've been learning.

30 DAYS TO TAMING YOUR FINANCES
What to Do (and Not Do) to Better Manage Your Money

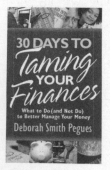

Giving readers the benefit of her many years' experience as a certified public accountant and certified behavioral consultant, Deborah Smith Pegues sheds light on the emotional and practical side of putting finances in order. The wealth of information readers will gather includes how to

- forget past financial mistakes and start fresh
- stop emotional spending and still be content
- fund future objectives with confidence

Each day's offering will inspire and motivate readers to savor the freedom that comes with organizing, valuing, and sharing their resources wisely.

30 DAYS TO A GREAT ATTITUDE
Strategies for a Better Outlook on Life

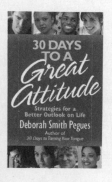

In this insightful guide, Deborah Smith Pegues uses biblical and modern-day examples to help you recognize and overcome such counterproductive behaviors as expecting failure, putting down someone else's success, being indifferent to the needs of others, and criticizing the conduct or choices others make.

Scripture-based principles, heart-searching personal challenges, and healing prayers and affirmations will help you conquer those bad attitudes that can derail your personal and professional relationships and point you toward the path to a new attitude.

30 DAYS TO TAMING YOUR STRESS

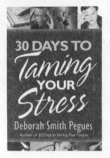

Are you sleeping well at night? Finding enough time in the day to do the things you enjoy? Sometimes stress causes us to miss out on the rest, fun, and health we long for. But you truly can tame this unruly taskmaster in 30 short days.

With insight gleaned from her experience as a behavioral consultant, Deborah Smith Pegues will help you learn how to change self-sabotaging behavior, enjoy the present, evaluate your expectations, and release your tension.

CONFRONTING WITHOUT OFFENDING

Deborah Smith Pegues shows clearly how confrontation, when done right, can be a powerful tool for mending broken relationships and for personal growth. Through her insights, you'll discover:

- whether to confront, when to confront, and which words to use
- how various personality types handle conflict
- the power of constructive criticism
- how to minimize defensiveness and hostility

Confronting Without Offending will give you the tools you need to restore peace and harmony to even the most troubled relationships at home, at work, and in any social setting.

EMERGENCY PRAYERS
God's Help in Your Time of Need

We need God's help...and fast! Deborah Smith Pegues offers us a 9-1-1 prayerbook for life's many circumstances and needs. Brief, immediate, and heartfelt, these prayers bring God's Word to the forefront of our minds as we lift up cries for

- help on the homefront
- financial discipline and direction
- resistance of temptations
- guidance in important decisions
- comfort in the midst of pain

This conveniently sized emergency guide can remain close at hand and heart as it leads us to God's presence for every need.

SOCIALLY SMART IN 60 SECONDS
Etiquette Do's and Don'ts for Personal and Professional Success

Deborah Smith Pegues offers 60-second etiquette solutions for awkward pauses, social situations, and everyday encounters. While other books focus on doing things right, Deborah shares how to do the right thing as she presents simple ways for us to

- make proper and inviting introductions
- give gifts for any occasion graciously
- scribe personable emails, letters, and thank-you notes
- understand and be mindful of intercultural do's and don'ts
- host events, dinners, and overnight guests with ease and generosity

For everything from networking to dating to tipping, this quick and thorough guide helps us turn our thoughts to the needs of others and practice courtesy and consideration anytime.